A Friend Remembers . . .

In her own moving account, Gilda Radner told the story of the last, bittersweet days of her life. Now one of her closest friends offers a warm and perceptive memoir of the years that came before.

David Saltman gave Gilda her first job in show business, as the campus radio station's wacky weather girl, when they met at the University of Michigan in 1965. They remained close for the rest of Gilda's life—through her days with Second City, her frenetic celebrity career with "Saturday Night Live," and her final years of genuine love and tragic illness.

In this affectionate yet well-balanced portrait, Saltman reveals the deeply troubled aspects of the comedian's life while also capturing her irrepressible comic spirit.

Saltman's work has appeared in *Rolling Stone*, the *New York Times*, and many other publications. He has worked as a writer and producer for PBS, ABC TV, and CBS TV's "Sunday Morning with Charles Kuralt."

GILDA

An Intimate Portrait

DAVID SALTMAN

CB
CONTEMPORARY
BOOKS

Library of Congress Cataloging-in-Publication Data

Saltman, David, 1946–
Gilda : an intimate portrait / David Saltman.
p. cm.
ISBN 0-8092-4102-1 (cloth)
0-8092-3815-2 (paper)
1. Radner, Gilda. 2. Comedians—United States—Biography. I. Title.
PN2287.R218S25 1992
792.7'028'092—dc20
[B] 92-3831
CIP

Excerpt from "Goodbye, Saccharin" reprinted with permission from National Broadcasting Company, Inc.

Published by Contemporary Books, Inc.
180 North Michigan Avenue, Chicago, Illinois 60601
Manufactured in the United States of America
International Standard Book Number: 0-8092-4102-1 (cloth)
0-8092-3815-2 (paper)

To Isa, Karina, and Sam, with love

Contents

Acknowledgments

The bulk of this book is firsthand reporting.

Direct quotations where I was present are written as best I remember them or can reconstruct them.

Direct quotations where I was not present are as reported to me by eyewitnesses and participants, or as reported in interviews as Gilda's own words, or quoted directly from her writings. Attributions for previously published material are given in the text.

In some cases the exact wording of Gilda's stories is an amalgam of the story as she told it to me and as she told it to a reporter. She was a performer above all and often "tried out" her stories and lines on her friends until she got them right. And she was known to edit in an artful manner.

As noted in the text, for some details of the history of the "Saturday Night Live" program, I am indebted to Doug Hill and Jeff Weingrad and their excellent book, *Saturday Night.*

Likewise, thanks, a bend of the elbow, and a tip of the hat to Tony Hendra for his insights and investigations into the history of American comedy and the legacy of the loudmouth. His book *Going Too Far* is a wealth of information and an invaluable guide.

To Gene Wilder I owe a debt of gratitude for his encouragement in going on with this book by helping me clarify my motives for writing it.

To Michael and Henrietta Radner, love, blessings, and peace.

To Kitty, Ellen, Pat, and many other old friends of Gilda's, love and thanks for reminiscing with me. You are all the best people in the world.

1

A Special Relationship

"Written in the way she really talked"

"HELLO, DAVE, IT'S ME, GILLIS."

"If you say 'Bunny! Bunny!' on the first day of every month, you'll have good luck and all your wishes will come true."

"Well, I'll be a monkey's coat!"

These fragments of Gilda's speech haunt me now. I can still hear her voice, her laugh. . . .

"Where's Dave? Why isn't Dave here?" Gilda Radner once wailed to some mutual friends. "I've known him for half my life!"

Gilda was my friend for nearly as long as I can remember. We first met as students and became fast friends, then lifetime confidants, for reasons and under circumstances you're about to share. I had the good fortune to observe and participate in much of her adult life firsthand.

How indubitably joyful it was to know her. How indelibly sad her cruel, painful death made me feel. I still cannot accept that she is no longer here, that, as another of her closest friends put it, "she had the nerve to die."

This book is an attempt to bring her back to life. It is an effort to remember her the way she wanted to be remembered—for her comedy, not her cancer.

When Gilda was sixteen years old, she worked as a junior counselor at her beloved summer camp, Camp Tamakwa. Her friends remember that "the little kids followed her around like ducks following their mother." She was, from an early age, a Pied Piper, whose bait was not sweet flute music but the ever sweeter music of laughter.

"I never laughed so hard in my life," one of her former camp followers recalls. "I always wanted to be with her, because I knew I would be laughing all day long."

Long before she became famous, Gilda was the kind of friend who inspired a cozy, crazy, childish possessiveness. You wanted her with you. She wanted you with her. When she was with you, she was always one hundred percent there, yours, eyeball to eyeball, including that brown sleepysand she loved to ridicule and roll between her fingers until it disappeared. When she was gone, there was an emptiness.

Gilda was full of sparkle and love, and that love extended in all directions, in the form of affection and humor, hoping and grateful and working hard for reciprocation.

As she grew older and more famous, she became more conscious of the work she had put in. She knew she inspired love in her friends, but she became a little warier of false love attracted by her wealth and position. As she put it at the height of her fame, with her customary blinding truthfulness:

"Dave, I'm an aging Jewess!"

"No, Gilda, you're still young and beautiful," I said, meaning every word.

"No, Dave, let's face it," she continued in a weary voice. "I'm just a Jewish girl from Detroit. Now when a guy looks at me, I don't know if he's thinking he'd like to get to know me, take me out, and maybe build a life together—or maybe he's thinking I look a lot like that girl on television," she said wistfully.

"Fame changes a lot of things," she said on another occasion, "but it can't change a light bulb."

As a defense against the snares and delusions of fame she frequently fell back to being her old, simple self with her old, trusted friends, those who had always been there kibitzing and holding the stool for her while she changed the light bulb herself.

Once, in her newly redecorated office at Rockefeller Center, she was in a pensive mood, meditating on all this, reflecting on the vicissitudes that had transformed her from plump young cowgirl of Camp Tamakwa to slender cover girl of *Rolling Stone.*

"You knew me when I was nothing and stuck with me when no one else cared, Dave," she said.

"You really were always there," she added, with a note of wonder in her voice.

She sounded amazed that anyone would put up with her peculiar life, so full of, as she said in another context, "dips and turns and kinks and spinarounds."

But as was her wont, she was exaggerating for dramatic effect. First of all, she had never been "nothing." And second, she had a solid handful of old friends who had stuck with her through fat and thin. We all felt part of her family: Dibby, her surrogate mother; Ellen, Kitty, Judy, and Pam, her spiritual sisters; I loved her like a brother, as did John Belushi, Bill Murray, and others you'll meet in these pages.

Gene Wilder, who truly loved her as a husband, has observed:

"Everyone I know who knew her and everyone I've

heard of who knew her had a special relationship with Gilda."

Indeed, Gilda had this unique effect on people. She was really *able* to create an oxymoronic "special relationship with everyone." Throughout her life she inspired intimacy. This is an extremely rare trait.

As an adult, Gilda was slender to skinny, above middle height, with an abundant tangle of brown hair surrounding a small, elongated, flexible face that could run the gamut from stunningly attractive to repulsively ugly. She was able to encompass a whole universe of expression in that face. A sharp-eyed fan once said Gilda looked like a second-grader who has just been told she can have a puppy and is pleased as pie, but who's also been told that her puppy won't live and can't understand why. She was once aptly described as "a thirty-three-year-old woman who appears to have a Band-Aid on her knee." Her even white teeth and winning smile were the finest product of the dental technician's grindstone. She had a uniquely peculiar wibble-wobbling walk that was once likened to " a chicken walk on tiptoes." She had kind, honest brown eyes that could turn small and smart or large and seductive, as necessary.

Her favorite clothing she herself described as "whatever's clean," adding, "Also, I think clothes should make you feel safe. I like clothes you could want to go to sleep in. I sometimes stand in front of the mirror and change a million times because I know I really want to wear my nightgown. . . ."

When once asked about her preference in shoes, she said: "Shoes that make your feet look cute, like puppy paws. And I like high heels, if they make your legs look long. A guy once told me I had long legs, so I capitalized on them by wearing high heels. Unfortunately, I also have a small head. I guess you shouldn't really upset the balance of nature, 'cause the longer I make my legs, the smaller my head looks—kind of like a little mountain peak off in the distance."

That small head was full of brains. Anyone who met her, even for the first time, could feel the force of her wit and intelligence. More than that, you could feel the results of an indefinable conscious inner "something" that had grown in her after her father's death.

Gilda cast a net of intimacy over her millions of fans, as well as her personal friends. Audiences genuinely loved her. On television, in the theater, and in print Gilda leapt off screen, stage, and page into the hearts of her viewers and readers. In real life and on television, she transcended time and space to touch nearly everybody in the same way with volcanic, loudmouthed, and frighteningly truthful bursts of humanity, humor, and pathos.

Unlike most of us, Gilda had no fear of revealing her innermost self. On the contrary, she milked it for all it was worth. With the sure intuition of a sage, she knew that what was true was also funny, if said quickly enough and with a certain intonation. Her fear was of rejection, of loss, of separation. This pathetic undercurrent created the winsomeness that reverberated in the hearts of everyone who loved her humor.

Gilda always identified herself clearly as "of her time"—a reluctant Bohemian during the sixties, a sudden "star" in the seventies, and ultimately a tragic heroine for the eighties. Meanwhile, she wore forever the mantle of Lucille Ball, Charlie Chaplin, and Jonathan Swift.

Gilda's fascinating story encompasses more than just the life of a complex, brilliant woman and her charmed circle of friends. It is the tragicomedy of a true, original, daring, and often tormented artist who had the courage to fly to the sun and the curse to melt at the zenith.

After she died, I longed to hear her musically scratchy, squinty voice again, her unique cackling laugh, her special way of saying "Oh, Gyahd!" and "Am I happy now?" and "Is that funny? Why is that funny?" Even though she understood better than anyone what was funny, she never stopped trying to see the humor in her life, and using it to lift ordinary experience to a sublime level.

Remembering Gilda prompted me to write—to write down things she said, her facial expressions, her body language, meals she ate, every diet she tried, every amusing, sad, or silly incident I could remember or find out about. At first this book was an assortment of miscellaneous pages full of notes, sketches, tales, punch lines. Then, as I began to contact mutual friends, just to talk about old times, to remember Gilda, or to verify this date or that story, the pages and tales began to take shape.

Everyone recalled something funny Gilda had said, something she had done, someone she had helped. For a while I thought I was writing a comic novel, along the lines of that old but not entirely forgotten classic *Zuleika Dobson*, where the overwhelming essence of the title character stands like a mighty oak as the center of the book and the unlikelihood of the plot—in this case Gilda's actual life—can be excused.

On these pages I wanted to hear Gilda laugh again. I was determined not simply to recite a litany of facts, beginning with the obligatory "She was born in Detroit on June 28, 1946. . . ." The result, for better or worse, is not really a biography, not a comic novel, but something else: a memoir, a paean, a meditation, a prayer.

She herself has written beautifully and movingly of her

monumental struggle between life and death. This book is a tribute to her life, which prepared her to face so bravely "the bourn from which there are no reruns."

It is, above all, a wish for the peace of her soul, finally at rest with the God she always believed in, felt part of, occasionally railed at, and valiantly struggled to understand.

"Writing in the way she really talked," I hope to recapture some of the flavor of Gilda's life. Along the way we will bump into funny phrases, funny people, silly situations. Perhaps somewhere, as our bellies are shaking from a good laugh, we will be lucky enough to discover "meaning" in her life, so short, so beautiful in its bright intensity, its tragicomic completeness.

Gilda probably would hate that sentiment and turn it into a joke. When she was sick, Gilda fought against being thought of as tragic in any way. She wanted to be just what she had always been—a jester, a comedian.

"It wasn't as if I was a dramatic actress associated with great tragic roles," she wrote in the book that soon proved posthumously what a tragic figure she was.

"Everything was working against me, but I wasn't going to accept that fate," she continued.

"I would be funny again."

She fulfilled this prophecy, reappearing on television after forcing cancer into retreat. It took place on "It's Gary Shandling's Show," and Gilda entered the scene to a standing ovation, whereupon she held her hands over her head like a winning prizefighter—in fact, just like Sly Stallone in one of her favorite movies, *Rocky*.

Daringly honest as ever, she successfully told cancer jokes. A new door opened in her mind. It was a fantastic performance, Gilda Daedalus.

As she herself had put it years earlier: "A person would

have to be an . . . an *asshole* . . . not to like *Rocky*!"

Gilda helped to shape her extraordinary era, even more than the era shaped her. For her life is the true story of the "Big Chill" generation. Lawrence Kasdan, who wrote that movie, also went to the University of Michigan. In fact, every time any of the old crowd saw that film the instant reaction was "Just like dinner at Kitty's." Later you'll meet Gilda's old friend Kitty.

So, where to begin? Gilda was my friend for nearly as long as I can remember. We were confidants for more than half her life, and I had the good fortune to observe and participate in much of her adult life firsthand.

She often introduced me to her new best friends:

"This is Dave. He saved my life!"

As she recounts in her memoir, *It's Always Something,* I was the guy who pulled her out of the path of a speeding car in Paris in 1966. More than friends and companions from then on, we had a bond even death could not break.

2

How I Saved Gilda's Life

"They pee in the middle of the sidewalk here"

PARIS. SUMMER, 1966. CLEAR EARLY MORNING. THE STREETS are alive with the smell of coffee and fresh bread. Beautiful girls in their summer dresses and state-of-the-art underwear stroll from shop to shop, buying here baguettes, there coffee beans, elsewhere pyramid-shaped containers of fresh milk.

I observe all this closely because I fancy myself as young Hemingway. Already a part-time correspondent for the *New York Times* and the *National Observer* and only incidentally a university junior on summer vacation, I spend the days in cafés, the nights on the *rues* and *ruelles* of the Latin Quarter, keeping eyes, ears, and pants open, learning there is more to life than what you see on Walter Cronkite.

Any day now, my girlfriend, Elena, and my secret love, Gilda, roommates from Ann Arbor, will arrive. They, on their first trips to Europe, will be coming by train from Brussels to the Gare du Nord.

Like Hemingway and the other hero of my daydreams,

Picasso, I already have attracted an adoring entourage of two towheaded college guys even more gullible than I, who actually believe, here in the mid-sixties, that I *am* young Hemingway. Moreover, they continually say so, in a fawning manner I find rather agreeable. For them, I can do no wrong. They are especially agog that, horny as we all are, I am about to meet not one but *two* reportedly gorgeous pieces of meat.

Finally the appointed day has arrived. Escorted by the entourage, I go early to the Gare du Nord. We have coffee. My blonder companion, John, remarks, for the hundredth time, "You really *are* just like Hemingway!" He is wrong. I do not yet have a mustache.

At the given hour the Brussels train pulls into the station. Gilda and Elena step off, resplendent in their youthful glows of beauty. They have, between them, eleven tons of luggage, which my two sidekicks carry, five-and-a-half tons apiece. I need my arms free to put around the waists of both girls.

At that time Gilda was what I would consider a perfect weight for her—ever so slightly on the meaty side. On the outside she was a typical Jewish ingenue from the Midwest. But on the inside she was very untypical: she was an ingenue who does not fancy herself beautiful and becomes even more beautiful because of her ingenuousness.

Humor was already her strongest feature. She had learned early that she got attention, especially attention from boys, by being funny. She also instantly fell in love with anyone who made her laugh.

She had up to now led a peculiar but relatively sheltered existence, as then befit wealthy Detroit Jewesses, who rarely ventured more than nine miles from the Park Shelton Hotel. She had decided to go to Europe at the last minute, tagging along with Elena, hoping to find romance in romantic Paris.

Elena is a similar type in some ways, also a Detroit Jewish-American princess, but she is already well traveled, having moved to Detroit with her immigrant parents via Argentina and Montreal. Elena is a good traveler. She is radiant, dying to speak French and eat *pâté de campagne*.

Gilda, by contrast, appears pale and wan, which is unusual for her. She is now feeling quite airsick, carsick, and trainsick. Her first words are delivered with a stomachachy sniff:

"Where can you get Pepto-Bismol in this *Paris*?"

I laugh.

"Gillis," I say, using one of my nicknames for her. "You are now in the land of the baguette. Forget Pepto-Bismol and every other American thing. There is nothing that real French bread and ultrawonderful French butter cannot cure," I say heartily.

Her stomach appears to do a wavy dance, and she makes a Lisa Loopner face, all frowny with a small, sad mouth. Of course none of us knew it was a Lisa Loopner face in those days. It was just a very Gilda face.

"No, I think I need Pepto-Bismol," she says through her nausea.

Turning to the entourage, who, burdened by luggage, can barely keep up with us, I say:

"Do you guys know any place with Pepto-Bismol?"

"What?" John asks, not believing he heard correctly.

"Pepto-Bismol. Gilda wants some Pepto-Bismol."

"There's that place called Le Drugstore," John's pal, Joey, offers. "On the Champs Elysées."

We decide to drop off the luggage and then search for Pepto-Bismol. We walk through the Faubourg St Denis to the river. We stroll the ageless streets that retain the purple hue of their glorious past. The entourage doesn't seem to notice any of this atmosphere. John and Joey are continually looking at each other and at us with eyes as big as silver dollars, as if they have never seen women before.

In half an hour we cross the Pont des Arts, and we turn into the rue de Seine. The wet cobblestones of the rue de Seine give off a strong scent of fish, which permeates the infamous Hôtel Welcome, where we are billeted. The hotel's motto in these days is "We get the writers on the way up and again on the way down."

It is an old and bravely repainted building that looks as if it has resisted time and tide since Rabelais. Inside, the hotel seems bare, as if all the furniture had been stolen except what could not fit in a van. The entourage unmoors the luggage from bent-over backs. Practically bowing, scraping, and walking backward out the door, they take leave and beetle off to their own, even worse, hotel.

In the Welcome's faded lobby Gilda whispers urgently to Elena. Elena, in turn, whispers urgently to the concierge. The concierge takes Gilda by the hand to the courtyard and points out the privy.

Like many of the no-star hotels in Paris in these days, the Welcome has only outdoor rest room facilities. Like most toilets in Paris, it is a Turkish two-footer: a ground-level hole in the porcelain flanked by two foot-shaped risers. Gilda is not so good at cross-cultural ergonomics, and she grew up in a really *nice* hotel, so she fails to appreciate the skill, study, and tradition that have gone into the placement of that hole. She does not for a moment consider the deleterious effects on health and posture of sitting for hours a week on a Seville Hotel "Comfort Throne." All she can do is wail.

"Eleeeeennnnna! Come and take a look at this . . . this . . . *dumper*!" she screams.

Elena is more or less of like mind, but what can they do? They do not have the stomach to search for a better class of fleabag, at least not right now, with nature calling like mad.

Just as Gilda has screwed up her courage and is about to enter the women's privy, two men come out of the men's. Both are adjusting their flies for more than the maximum allowable time, and one of them, staring straight at Gilda, although with half-closed eyes, slowly and half-consciously strokes his crotch. Gilda is also staring, her habitual expression in those days. She quickly tears her eyes away, enters the water closet, and expresses through all nine vents.

Afterward, the concierge shows us to our room and explains the presence of a candle, which we find on the dresser, along with a few matches. This is the emergency kit. If, during the night, Gilda or Elena is summoned again by the call of nature, she is to arise from bed and feel around until she has located the matches. Lighting the candle, she will hurry through the hall and down the stairs, holding the candle in one hand and shielding the flickering flame with the other. This is necessary, our concierge explains, because when she reaches the back door and steps nimbly out into the night, a playful gust of wind sometimes snuffs out the candle. If this were to happen, she would find herself standing in a strange courtyard in total darkness.

We thank the concierge for her enlightening explanations and hurry from the hotel back into the *bruit* of the Left Bank. Forgetting about most of our bodily functions, we recall that we are young and in Paris. What could be more romantic?

We head for the Right Bank, Le Drugstore, and Pepto-Bismol. As we reach the Champs Elysées, Gilda suddenly queries:

"Why are all the men masturbating?"

In spite of her nausea, her powers of observation are unerring. For the first time I notice that most of the men not dressed in expensive suits are continually holding, rubbing, massaging, cupping, palming, scratching, stroking, or playing with their *zezis.* Why, indeed? Is France not only the land of love but also the land of lice? Or are they just glad to see us? Judging from the glazed looks in their eyes, the action is mostly unconscious. But who can tell? They're French after all. Very Latin.

We realize we are unable to answer her question without a great deal more fieldwork, so we proceed to the Place de la Concorde and turn left toward Le Drugstore. I am pointing out all the historic sights and beautiful vistas, pontificating on the French sensibility. Elena is purring their lovely language, reading signs and asking directions in elegant French from passersby. She is in her element, busily translating everything written and spoken, her four-years-of-high-school-two-years-of-college-and-a-bit-of-Montreal French finally getting a workout.

"And what's that *smell?*" Gilda asks abruptly as we pass a *pissoir.* "Eckhkh! It's *piss*! I'm gonna throw up!"

Her hand flies to her face, and she dry-heaves a couple of times. We hurry toward Le Drugstore. Poor Gilda is in misery, her stomach paining her, her nose grossing her out, and her ears offended by the loose-lipped slurrings of an alien tongue.

Though brand-new, Le Drugstore is already the rage of Paris. The French workers and customers there are delighted to see some Americans for a change. Not until a year from now, with the Vietnam War in sudden crescendo, will Americans be spat on in Paris and cursed with the terrible phrase *"Amerloques! Assassins!"*

Elena asks the Drugstore people if they have Pepto-Bismol. She translates: "Pep-TO Bis-MOL." They have, at six times what it costs in Ann Arbor. Gilda buys a month's supply, paying in dollars. Her purse runneth over with bottles of pink liquid and tablets. We go to the nearest café, Fouquet's, where she orders water, or rather Elena does for her. Elena has coffee, I *un rouge*, which I have just learned how to say.

"Dave, do you actually *like* this Paris?" Gilda inquires, stirring her pink drink. "It's so different—so hectic and weird. They pee in the middle of the sidewalk here!"

"Of course, it's different," Elena says. "We're in Europe now."

Gilda is having a hard time with the difference. She has been to Florida a dozen times, various spots in Ontario eight or nine times, and New York half a dozen times, but it usually rained four days out of five.

Elena, on the other hand, is already practically foreign, but in a very American way. She is already fluent enough in Spanish to call herself bilingual, and she's quite good in French. She is feeling no pain in Paris and certainly having none of Gilda's.

Gilda takes a test sip of her pink mineral water.

"Eeuu. It has gas." She makes a face and drinks anyway.

The Bismol calms her stomach a bit, and she is finally, bravely, ready to give Paris a go. Elena votes to head straight for the Louvre, but Gilda is not ready for such a large dose of culture right off the bat. She is ready for a meal.

"Let's have lunch," Gilda says, "at one of those famous French cafés."

I know about the Dôme and the Deux Magots from my impersonation of Hemingway, so I suggest we try one of those.

"Deux Magots. What does that mean?" Gilda asks.

"Two maggots," Elena translates.

"What? Why would they name a restaurant for two maggots? Or maybe I don't want to know," she adds. "Let's just have lunch here."

As we're sitting there, a man leaves the *pissoir*. He stares at Gilda, who is, as usual, also staring. He begins playing with himself. Gilda looks away, and her mouth squinches to a tiny O the size of a Cheerio.

"So how was your trip?" I ask innocently.

"It was great," Elena says.

"Disgusting," Gilda complains simultaneously, hissing through the O of her mouth. "That stupid Icelandic takes forever, and you have to sit twelve abreast, and the plane always leans to whatever side the stewardess is on!"

They had arrived in Paris after stopping in Iceland and then spending a few days in Luxembourg, Brussels, and Amsterdam, the infamous "Icelandic Route." Along with thousands of other teenage adventurers, I had done the same myself a couple of weeks earlier.

"In Amsterdam I got diarrhea in the lobby of the Rembrandt museum, and I never saw even one painting," Gilda continues, "because I got so grossed out at the Anne Frank House. And the soap in the youth hostel had pubic hair on it!

"Yuck!"

Always trying to profit from her pain, Gilda later wove that pubic hair into a Roseanne Roseannadanna sketch.

Elena laughs. "Gilda has been having a hard time," she allows.

"And Elena hates me 'cause I'm always saying 'Huh?' 'What?' 'What did they say?' She wants to kill me." Gilda smiles.

Elena does not deny this. "You just have to wait 'til they've finished talking before you ask me what they're saying, 'cause otherwise I can't hear them myself."

"I can't help it. I feel lost not knowing the language. The

only thing I know in a foreign language is '*Nardo morte.*' "

"*Nardo morte?*" I ask. "What's that?"

"It means 'Bernardo is dead,' " Gilda says. "That's what they say in *West Side Story* when Bernardo dies. '*Nardo morte.*' Or something like that."

We laugh.

Just then the waiter comes and unleashes a volley of impertinent-sounding French.

"What did hc say?" Gilda asks.

"Just a minute," Elena says impatiently. "He's asking what you want to eat."

"Do they have tuna fish?" she inquires.

We do not know how to ask for tuna fish in French, so we end up ordering *croque-monsieurs,* which turn out to be grilled cheese sandwiches with a college education.

Over the sandwiches, Gilda continues her tale of woe in Amsterdam.

"So I was leaning over this canal, trying to see into one of those houseboats, when my billfold dropped out of my purse and fell into the water. It just floated away, and I was standing there, helpless, billfoldless, screaming. And even though everybody in fucking Amsterdam speaks English, nobody could help me, and I lost all my traveler's checks. And then it took me the whole next day just to find the American Express office!"

Gilda's poor-little-rich-girl intonation and facial expressions make Elena and me laugh heartily. And even Gilda sees some glimmer of humor and finally laughs herself.

After eating the *croque-monsieurs,* we walk toward the Louvre.

In those days, a scant twenty-five years past, it was still possible to visit Paris for no more than five dollars a day, room and three meals included, with even a little left over for a Métro ticket to the Louvre (admission free). We, of course, do not take the Métro, preferring to rely on one of the tried-and-true five-dollar-a-day dicta: as they say in French, *numéro onze*, old "number eleven," known in England as shank's mare.

As we are standing outside the Louvre, Gilda has a stomach-flash of the Rembrandt museum and decides she does not want to go inside after all. She wants to see some sights first, spend the day outdoors, walking in this beautiful city. Elena is determined, so she goes to the Louvre alone. Agreeing to rendezvous with Elena later, Gilda and I commence prowling the streets of Paris.

We wander from the Louvre back onto the Left Bank, into the crawling swirl of the rue de Buci. The bars are wide open. Bicycles line the curb. Meat and vegetable markets are in full bloom. We dodge pigs on hooks and newspaper funnels full of flowers. The streets around here twist and turn like a worm on drugs. Food is everywhere, and every woman we see, except Gilda, has at least one vegetable under each arm.

We pass the Eglise St Germain-des-Prés and inspect the defenestrated gargoyles littering the garden. On the benches are snoozing even scarier, human gargoyles—droolers, honkers, what-have-you. They'll arise at dinnertime to prowl these ancient lanes, jaws jutting like their stone counterparts, hungry to have a history.

Gilda seems glazed. She is feeling jet lag on top of her nausea, and she is generally weirded out by the strange new sights, smells, and sounds. Her lens is always open, her brain is always taping, but in these early days she has not yet learned how to process the new, odd impressions she is constantly taking in.

I had been to Paris for a couple of weeks the summer before, feeling just the way she does now. But it had completely changed my life. What I had previously thought beautiful and fine I now regarded as tawdry and ugly. What I had previously seen as horrible and degraded now appeared noble and true. There was nowhere in Paris more picturesque to me than, for instance, a courtyard in the squalid rue Cloître du Notre-Dame, on the Ile de la Cité. Reached through a low passageway, it is an oblong court formed by a rectangle of ancient buildings. They are so decrepit they appear to have imploded, to the extent that a loud sneeze would probably cause them to crumble into dust. The ground of the courtyard is slippery with slime and congealed pigeon dung. Cinders and garbage line the crevices. Pale, bony street urchins squawk through perennial games of soccer played with a balled-up rag in better shape than their clothes. The smell of mildew is everywhere.

"Ah, Europe," I breathe as we pass the *église*, ignoring the grotesque monstrousness of the scene, seeing only something different from the disgustingly familiar middle-class streets and alleys of Akron, Ohio. Gilda, however, does not share my mental regrooving.

"Dave, this is gross," she says, gesturing at the droolers. "Let's get out of here."

After a walk that makes our muscles ache, we return to the Louvre and meet Elena, shimmering with the vibrations of a thousand years of culture.

She is ravenous for dinner, as are we all. We embark for a restaurant.

Another five-dollar-a-day secret, dovetailing with number eleven and staying at the incomparable Hôtel Welcome, was dining at student bistros around the rue Mouffetard, behind the Panthéon.

In the ethos of those mid-sixties, the charm of Paris did not lie in its exquisite dining rooms, like Le Train Bleu or La Tour d'Argent, but rather in genuine, authentic holes-in-the-wall, those unknown bistros of the Left Bank where a Vietnamese or Arab concoction could be consumed, hair and all, for seventy-five cents including tip.

So after this trying day, in which Pepto-Bismol had not been economized, and because I felt a certain responsibility as guide, having been in Paris a previous summer and an entire week longer than Gilda and Elena, in my wisdom that evening I decided it was in the rue Mouffetard area that the two charming ladies and I should dine.

And that is why as the sun is going down Gilda, Elena, and I find ourselves treading the dark districts behind the Panthéon, hurrying to find a street so small it is just a two-letter abbreviation in my battered red copy of *Paris par Arrondissement.*

The rue Mouffetard, like the adjacent streets, runs between the boulevard St-Germain and the boulevard St-Michel, roughly parallel to the latter but of a completely different character. Later, like the Marais and other former slums of Paris, this area, and especially the Place de la Contrescarpe, would become "gentrified." But in these days the narrow streets, dark and muddy, took on a mysterious aura at night. Trades that did not wear fig leaves were carried on. Coming from the bright lights of the boulevard du Montparnasse or the "Boul Mich," where there are always well-dressed crowds, strangers who ventured behind the Panthéon would be seized by gloom and terror. There you were suddenly plunged into an intricate network of dark, dank passages and *passerelles* that surround, and are surrounded by, that bright aura of civilization, reflected in the sky itself.

In the heart of this demimonde, only at wide intervals do you find a pale street lamp casting a smoky light. Through the thick shadows in between, we walk quickly, the tapping of our heels echoing ominously for blocks. Most shops are shut; the ones still open at night are of dubious character: a dirty wine shop without lights, a store that sells dust-covered vials of eau de cologne. Even the weather conditions are changed in this strange district: it is cold in the summer and warm in the winter.

Shivering, Gilda and Elena look at each other with widening eyes as I usher them down one evil-smelling lane after another.

"Couldn't we just eat at that café again?" Gilda moans, even though the *croque-monsieurs* made her stomach hurt and she had vowed never even to look at cheese again.

"No, no," I insist. "You deserve a good French dinner. And I hear this place has atmosphere."

"Even Mars has an atmosphere," Gilda says doubtfully, "but I don't want to eat *there* either."

"Listen, Gilda, you need to visit a place where real Parisians go, not just these guidebook places that end up full of American tourists."

Indeed, more than once we had pretended to be Canadian to avoid the loud, seersucker-clad Americans who polluted most of the better five-dollar-a-day joints in Paris. Perhaps they avoided the rue Mouffetard because they were not up to this truly fearsome trek. In any case we, like a James Bond martini, shaken but not stirred, eventually reach our destination: the Impasse Bouvart and the front door of the highly touted and low-priced Crache & Péte, as I believe it was called.

The Crache & Péte stands, or perhaps *crouches* would be more accurate, in the aforementioned Impasse Bouvart, one of the tiniest of the capillaries in the body Parisian. The whole restaurant, including kitchen, is approximately the size of a Manhattan studio apartment.

Reservations are never needed here, even though there are only four tables. When occupied at all, it is invariably by the less affluent members of the Parisian English-speaking press—in other words, proofreaders at the *Herald Tribune*—or students or slumming tourists like us. It is one of the few restaurants that is avoided by even the dogs of Paris.

The proprietor and chef, M. Mot de Cambronne I believe was his name, was a fat-necked Frenchman with a huge boil on the side of his head. That night he was offering a prix fixe dinner for four francs. Eighty cents seemed a bit extravagant, but what the hell? We were in Paris after all. Why not splurge on a fine meal?

The first course consisted of a liquid masquerading as *potage*.

"This is great," Gilda said as she slurped through gritted teeth. "I think it's boiled tablecloth stains."

The second course bore a certain resemblance to raw green stuff.

Gilda said of it, with a grimace:

"Oh boy, my favorite. Chopped stocking salad!"

The main course consisted of braised crayfish shells on a bed of raw rice, accompanied by green beans overcooked to the point of extinction.

"God!" exclaimed Gilda when it arrived with its ungodly stench. "I think I'll stub out my cigarette in there before I eat it."

And for dessert you had a choice: Elena ordered the delightful *crème brulée*, which *was* burnt cream.

Gilda was in the mood for flaky French pastry.

When it came, she bit into the many crispy leaves and commented:

"Great, it's a baked calendar!"

The "meal" works its way through our respective systems even before we leave the restaurant. We line up three in a row for the use of the Turkish facilities.

That night we retire to our penthouse at the Hôtel Welcome. There is no *ascenseur.* It is a single room, or actually three-quarters of a room because of the sloping roof—one of the celebrated *toits de Paris.*

Despite the alfresco *toilette,* the hotel at least has a "bathroom" down the hall, in which there is an old cast-iron bathtub and a sink. You can take a cold bath anytime, but if you want a hot one you must order it from the concierge well in advance so that a fire can be lit in the hotel's ancient water heater. We request three baths, and when finally finished several hours later, we feel just about half-human once again.

Gilda puts on her favorite pink see-through nightgown and takes one of the two single beds. Elena and I undress in the dark and take the other.

Gilda burps.

"Good night," she says. "Please don't make love."

I say, "Good night."

"Don't worry, we won't," Elena says.

We all try to sleep.

After fifteen minutes, Gilda pipes up in a small voice: "Elena, I have to go to the bathroom."

Elena pretends to be asleep.

"Elena!" Gilda says louder. "I have to go to the bathroom! Elena! Dave!"

We cannot ignore this plea.

"Whuh?" Elena mutters, as if awakened. "So get the candle and go."

"Will you go with me?"

Elena sees instantly there is no denying this request. So she spreads the risk: "Dave, please. You come too."

I take in a bushelful of air and, exhaling, roll out of bed. We dress and take up candle and matches.

Mindful of the concierge's words, we take special care to cup our hands in front of the candle flame. Slowly, one step at a time, triple-file all the way, I holding the candle, they sheltering with their hands, we tiptoe out our door, down the hall, down several flights of stairs to the courtyard door. The management seems to have added a couple of flights during the night.

Slowly we open the latch and step out into the night. Sure enough, a wind blows up and immediately snuffs out the candle.

We are all suddenly standing in the middle of the blackest courtyard we have ever seen, on the darkest night in history.

As our eyes gradually adjust, we become aware of thousands of even darker shapes flitting about the courtyard. We don't know whether they are bats, birds, or alien spacecraft. The corners seem full of shadows and ominous foreign gleams that disappear when you look directly at them. We hear the roar of the river in the distance.

The sound of rushing water makes Elena and me want to pee as well. I can just go in the courtyard, and do, thank God, while the girls try to maneuver in the Turkish toilet. It is a very strange feeling to be standing in pitch blackness in a foreign city, peeing into the void and feeling the breeze off the river. I could only imagine, from the sounds, what poor Gilda and Elena were going through:

"Is the hole there?"

"I dunno. I can't see. What's the difference? Just go and get it over with."

"But I don't want to go on the floor."

"Ackkk! No!"

The sound of water spilling on the floor. The bumping of a bucket and clanking of metal on stone.

"Jesus, I'm gonna piss in my hat from now on!"

"You don't have a hat."

"Well, I'm gonna get one."

We finally make it back to the room. We all wash our hands and feet thoroughly in the sink and blissfully drop into our beds.

Despite our best intentions, Elena and I are still teens in heat, and some twenty minutes later there is a certain shuffling of sheets, creaking of boards, and no way to disguise that telltale sound, "Blorp."

Gilda pretends to snore.

A few moments later, as Elena and I are about to become blissfully unaware of anything, we suddenly hear a huge "Whump!"

We stop and peer into the darkness.

"Gillis?" I say tentatively.

"Nothing to worry about," Gilda answers in a stage whisper. "Just my robe falling on the floor."

"Your robe? Making a huge noise like that?"

"Yeah, well, I was inside it at the time!"

All three of us dissolve in laughter.

As quiet eventually descends once again, nature once more begins to take its course, and Gilda again pretends to snore.

At three o'clock in the morning, Gilda can stand it no longer.

"Can I get in bed with you guys?" she chirps suddenly. "I want to vomit all over you!"

Elena and I laugh. "Sorry, Gillis. We couldn't help it." Finally, we all sleep.

The next morning, through the undraped windows, long fingers of sunlight reach suddenly across the pale walls of our hotel room. We all wake up at the same time, with the same gnawing feeling in our bellies, a mixture of hunger and nausea. This hotel is so cheap it does not provide the customary continental breakfast, so after washing up we once again find ourselves outside, aboard number eleven, searching for a café.

We had heard about a student cafeteria on the boulevard St-Michel. Upon presentation of some sort of student identification, you could eat for less than a dollar and have something left over for bus fare. It is not far from the hotel, so we bend our steps toward the infamous Boul Mich.

The food there looks decent, but after our dinner last night Gilda is taking no chances.

She grabs Elena by the elbow and forces her to commit translation.

"What's that?" she says, pointing at a nice-looking salad featuring leaves that remind me of chicory or escarole.

"*Qu'est-ce que c'est?*" Elena asks the guy behind the counter.

"*Salade de pissenlit,*" the guy answers.

It is a word Elena is not familiar with, so she asks him to write it down. When Gilda takes a look at the slip of paper, she freaks.

"Piss-in-it salad? No, no! How can they piss in their salads?" she cries. "I gotta take a Pepto-Bismol." She rummages in her purse.

"Gillis, I'm sure it's not piss. I just don't know the word, that's all," Elena explains. But Gilda holds firm.

"I am not eating anything called 'piss-in-it,' " she declares, ordering, via Elena, a plain roll. She washes this down with a small bottle of Evian water with two pink tablets in it.

We spend the morning sightseeing. I have been studying various guidebooks, looking for the out-of-the-way place off the beaten tourist track.

"How about this? A tour of the sewers of Paris?"

"Dave, gross!" Gilda exclaims. She does a Lisa Loopner voice: "I didn't come to Paris to look at their sewwwers, for God's sake!"

"Well, actually, Gillis, the sewers of Paris have quite an interesting history. Known as *les égouts de Paris. . . .*"

I launch into tales of the French resistance, and Gilda is totally grossed out. The girls definitely veto visiting any sewers, regardless of how many Jews were saved. I am free to go on my own, they say.

So we stay above ground for the day, visiting the usual tourist attractions.

For lunch we again try a student café. The chief pull of this place is its enormous menu. Any of more than three hundred items can be purchased for less than the cost of a bus ride. We are all amazed at the variety on the menu and resolve, after lunch, to take a look at the huge kitchen that must be working day and night to prepare all these dishes.

The food itself is—well, *edible* would be too strong a word. But what can you do to steak and french fries? In any case, we are still amazed by the amount available. Under cover of visiting the bathrooms ("God forbid, knock wood, bite your tongue, pick your face"), Gilda, Elena, and I peek into the kitchen.

Instead of the dozens of chefs and sous-chefs we expect to see, there is only one very fat fellow in the kitchen, and he is sitting in a comfortable-looking chair reading a magazine. As an order comes in, this gentleman, without the slightest hurry, puts down the magazine, goes to the cupboard, and takes out a can. From another cupboard he takes another can. He mixes a little from each can into a pan. Heating the pan, he stirs the mix around a bit. He then transfers it to a plate and puts the plate on a rack. He then returns to the magazine.

We laugh out loud and leave.

We sightsee until our feet hurt. Finally, the dinner hour arrives.

For dinner that night we are desperate to avoid the Crache & Péte, the student cafés, and all restaurants of that ilk. By chance, through some friend of a friend, we manage to meet a genuine French person, a certain Jean-Claude. We ask his advice about where and what to eat. He tells us about a place that serves a wonderful (and of course very inexpensive) *raclette*, that Alsatian and French-Swiss delicacy so highly esteemed by Europeans with medium-sized pear-shaped breasts and slender racing waists.

We begin to salivate, as Gilda would say, like a horse with a sandwich in his tail.

It has become a warm, bright evening with streaks of sunset rippling through the sky. Snails are staying out of their shells past their bedtime. Men in berets walk down the street licking their mustaches, holding their groins. We walk past walls old and crumbling, hearing the pleasant sound of water trickling from the urinals into the Seine. As we pass, up bang shutters as little streams of rain and pisswater purl through ancient gutters.

The *raclette* place is in the seventh *arrondissement*, a centuries-old part of Paris in which the Eiffel Tower stands. Its sign, something like "La Raclure," is painted in large, curving bright red letters. It has red-and-white checked tablecloths, flowers, and a candle on each table.

"Finally," Gilda says, her face breaking into jubilation, "we're going to a decent restaurant. Thank God!" We are all quite hungry and very excited about the world-famous, unparalleled *raclette.* When the waiter comes, we can barely keep from drooling.

"We'll have your famous *raclette,* of course," I say with a smirk, in the best French I can muster: "*Nous aurons votre raclette fameuse, bien sûr.*"

The waiter winks, returns the smirk, and says, "*Bien sûr.*"

By now we *are* drooling for a taste of this nonpareil French delicacy.

"I can't believe that I, Gilda Susan Radner, am going to eat a *raclette,*" Gilda says, rolling the *r*s, starting to really get into it. "*What* is it again?"

We all sit in puzzled anticipation for an unconscionably long time.

Finally the waiter arrives, bearing a huge covered dish. We salivate in high gear. He puts the dish down on the table, removes the cover with a flourish, and reveals—the world-famous *raclette.*

Elena and I sit mesmerized. We see a marvelous small, yellow dairy confection. It is garnished with some sort of spicy vegetable.

Gilda sees the emperor is naked—and very, very tiny to boot.

"But . . . but . . . it's just a little piece of cheese melted onto a plate! With a pickle!" she exclaims.

Indeed it is. Suddenly the scales fall from our eyes. We have been frogswoggled. We are cheesed off. You give something a fancy French name. . . . If we hadn't had someone like Gilda along, we probably would have written home about it, raving about the wonderful *raclette de Paris,* thus guaranteeing that the culinary sins of the fathers be transmitted to the stomachs of the second, third, and fourth generations.

To keep to our five-dollar-a-day budgets, we are unable

to order anything besides this arch-strange dish called *raclette.* We eat it with bread and drink the house wine and water without gas (to which Gilda adds liberal quantities from her stash of Pepto-Bismol) and depart in a hurry after leaving a minuscule tip. *Service* has not even been *compris.*

Afterward, to help digest this truly inexpensive meal, we walk. Somehow we find ourselves in another eerie twilight district similar to the rue Mouffetard. We soon come upon a small square surrounded by dingy cafés. Dozens of people are milling about the square, all of uncertain character: our eyes are caught first by a man with sticking-plaster patches on his face and a long steel chain around his waist; another is dressed in a nun's habit; a third has skin full of enormous pockmarks, as if he had not quite recovered from smallpox. Practically on cue, all, including the nun, grab their groins when the girls appear on the scene.

The accumulation of bad food, weird grotesquerie, and a long, hectic day is too much for Gilda. She suddenly purses her lips and begins to walk very, very fast.

Elena and I practically run after her but do not catch up with her until the Pont de l'Archevêché. Puffing for breath, we cross behind Notre-Dame and then over onto the Right Bank.

The sight of Notre-Dame seems to calm Gilda down a bit, and, walking farther, more slowly this time, we all feel a little more cooled down, if a bit of indigestion doesn't bother you, by the time we reach the Champs Elysées.

At the Rond-Point, Gilda glances at the *pissoir* just in time to see two men putting their prongs back in.

As we approach the Arc de Triomphe, she notices four men walking abreast. Their right arms are around one another's shoulders, their left hands each "adjusting" their respective crotches.

She looks at Elena and me, who are hand in hand. It is obvious that Gilda again suddenly feels extremely strange. We are "a couple"; she is "the girl alone." Her feet hurt. She's lonely beyond measure, dying for a boyfriend, a date, someone to touch, a decent meal, a warm fire, her father, her brother, even her mother, the green, green grass of home.

Unfortunately, we learn all this only later, for right then, without warning, Gilda shrieks and runs right into the middle of the Champs Elysées!

She throws herself full-length onto the roadway.

Her brown hair blows in the wind as the cars whip around the Place de l'Etoile at ninety miles an hour, unaware that she is lying there and in any case not about to stop for a mere manic-depressive American tourist.

I cannot believe my eyes. Without thinking, I run into the road to rescue her. But she does not want to be rescued. She wants to get hit by a car!

"No, no, let me die here!" she insists, fighting me as I put one hand into her hair and the other around her waist and drag her, kicking and screaming, back onto the sidewalk. "I want them to hit me!"

"Gilda, are you out of your mind!?" I scream.

"Yes!" she shouts.

We struggle a bit, and then, as we reach safety, she abruptly wilts and changes her tone.

"At least someone cares about me," she says softly and gratefully. "Dave, you saved my life."

I am suddenly furious. "So now, Gillis, your ass belongs to me! Don't you ever *dare* try anything like that again!" I scold her. Elena is mute with shock.

"I can't believe how fast they drive," Gilda says in wonderment, in a completely different, surprised tone of voice.

We manage a nervous, false laugh, more of a relieved snort.

Breathless, tearful, and dispirited, we all return to the hotel. Exhausted, we all fall asleep with our clothes on.

The next day, Gilda goes to American Express—she finds it quickly this time—and spends a fortune booking a first-class Air France flight back to Detroit.

In all, Gilda's first, and nearly final, trip to Europe lasts just a little more than a week. She does not return until sixteen years later, in 1982, when she is madly in love with Gene Wilder and is finally ready to handle what she termed "the difference."

3

Ann Arbor Days and Nights

"You've heard me speak of Dibby"

THE FIRST TIME I LAID EYES ON GILDA WAS IN 1965, ELEVEN months before the events in Paris just described.

I was struggling with suitcases, clambering up the stairs of "the apartment" with Elena and my parents. It was the top floor of a delightful old gray shingled house with red trim and a turret at 725 Haven Street in Ann Arbor, Michigan. Soon, thanks to Gilda's whiplash wit and huge heart, 725 Haven became an oasis in the jumpy, intense Ann Arbor of the era, with its swirl of antiwar and civil rights activity. It was one of the few places in town where you could find humor, laughter, music, a good time.

That first day, when we came up the stairs, Gilda, her mother, Henrietta, and her brother, Michael, were in the living room. Ellen Frank was in the kitchen, already washing dishes and cleaning floors.

Gilda, Elena, and Ellen were approximately sophomores, and I was more or less a junior at the University of Michigan. With the university's peculiar trimester system, you were never quite sure what year you were in. Gilda had an especially hard time figuring it out because she never took a full load of courses. All Gilda knew was that she was majoring in oral interpretation and public speaking. And for the first time in her life, she was trying hard to be a little bit of a bad girl. This attempt had begun late the previous year when she had smuggled her girlfriend Judy into the dorm and made her stand on top of a toilet so an extra pair of feet would not show as a dorm board member passed through the bathroom. She had stayed out late in 1965, and the dorm board had said she'd have to stay in every weekend until June. So she had simply dropped out of school and returned in the summer. Gilda had learned early how to avoid conflict and still get what she wanted.

The girls were all roommates, and I was Elena's boyfriend.

Gilda was wearing a pink skirt and a white sweater. Her mother, as I recall, was speaking:

"And don't forget to eat from the four basic food groups, every day."

"I won't, Mom. Oh, look—Elena's here."

"Who's that guy with the suitcases? Is he Jewish?"

"Hi, Mrs. Radner. Hi, Gilda. This is my friend Dave," Elena introduced us, "and his parents, Dr. and Mrs. Saltman."

"This is my mom, Mrs. Herman Radner, and my brother, Mickey," Gilda said, precisely mimicking Elena's tone of voice and manner of expression.

"Charmed," said Henrietta. "Did you say 'doctor'? I have this pain. . . ."

When Mrs. Radner learned my father was merely a doctor of philosophy, she sniffed, stepped back a pace, and began to reexamine our clothes.

Gilda intervened.

"Let's eat," she said.

That had always been my solution to low-level conflict too. I could see we were going to get along great.

It was my first meal in the Haven Street kitchen. It was a big white kitchen that looked out onto a big yard. We sat at a white Formica table that had space for four adults or twenty teenage college students. I don't recall what we talked about that first time, probably college and majors and all sorts of serious stuff. But I do recall what we ate: Gilda's favorite food, tuna fish.

I don't like to think how many tuna had to be killed over the next couple of years so that kitchen table could become the center of the universe.

Sitting around that table, we learned that Gilda's childhood had not been easy, nor had her relations with her two remaining family members.

Gilda found some relief in telling us how she never got over the death of her father, Herman, a powerful businessman in a now-vanished Detroit of elegance and charm, when American wheels ruled the world.

Gilda's grandfather, né George Ratkowsky, had emigrated from Lithuania to New York City, where Herman and his ten siblings grew up on the Lower East Side. In 1906 the family moved to Detroit, where George lived for the next forty-eight years, during which time he became a wealthy kosher meat dealer. When George died, in November 1954 at age eighty-four, he was eulogized as "a prominent Jewish philanthropist," and Herman himself, a dutiful if somewhat wayward son, always took a keen interest in Jewish affairs and Jewish welfare.

As a young man, Herman Radner did not have much education, never having gotten past the fifth grade. But he was sharp, and he quickly realized that a young man who knew how to shoot a good game of pool would never go hungry in this world. So he hung out at a neighborhood pool hall and became a hustler, shooting straight pool and nine-ball with equal facility. After a while, he and his friends had won enough money to buy the pool hall.

By the 1920s, Herman and his syndicate were wealthy enough to buy a brewery. They chose the Walkerville Brewery in Windsor, Ontario, just across the river from Detroit and free from any of those pesky American Prohibition laws. By Repeal, Herman Radner was wealthy enough that family folklore tells how he was once the victim of an attempted kidnapping by rival bootleggers. Herman escaped down a dark alley, getting shot in the leg in the process.

Herman's wealth did not make him forget his humble origins. During the Depression, Herman turned his brewery into a free lunchroom for the poor, and he became indelibly known as a philanthropist, following his father's lead. Herman became one of the patrons of the Jewish old folks' home in Detroit and was listed in *Who's Who in American Jewry.*

On November 29, 1937, at age forty-four, Herman married the lovely Miss Henrietta Dworkin. Four years later Henrietta gave birth to Michael and five years after that to Gilda.

Gilda described herself as an "unhappy, fat, and mediocre" child. She has called her childhood "a nightmare." Its only high point lay in her relationship to her father.

It was Herman who first taught Gilda to sing and dance. He called her "my heart" when she performed for him, and when Gilda's army of relatives showed up, one platoon at a time, he would march out his little "butterball trouper" and put her through her paces.

Gilda's father used his own sense of humor to defuse his daughter's childhood temper tantrums. When she threw one, he would clap appreciatively and call her "Sarah Bernhardt."

One of Gilda's favorite pictures was taken when she was eight years old, at her brother's bar mitzvah in Detroit. Gilda, glassy-eyed, is dancing with her father. She is wearing a dark satin dress and petticoats; he is wearing black tie and looking as blissful as she.

She and Herman loved to go to the theater together in downtown Detroit. They would always sit in the third row, and Gilda was certain all the performers were looking directly at her. Years later, when she herself was performing on Broadway, she was stunned to find that when she looked out into the audience she was blinded by the lights and could not see a thing.

Gilda's father took her to her first Broadway productions at the old Riviera Theater: together they saw road shows of *Li'l Abner*, *Most Happy Fella*, and even *Rigoletto*. It was after one of these productions that Herman confided to his only daughter that he had never really wanted to become a business and real estate tycoon. His dream had always been to work as a song-and-dance man in the theater.

"He could have done it, too," Gilda said often.

"Some of his spunk must have come out in me, because he used to love to perform. He was funny. He was a good storyteller. He did magic tricks. He loved to sing, and he could tap-dance, and he couldn't carry a tray of food to the table without tripping to make us kids laugh and make my mother nervous. In the years that I've been performing I feel that some part of my father is back alive in me, back doing what he always wanted to do."

Her father loved corny jokes, and he used to love to watch her perform, calling her "my little ham" to alternate with "my heart."

If he could not be a Broadway showman, Gilda's father did the next-best thing. After selling the brewery, he bought one of the best hotels in Detroit, the Seville, which had a small theater in it and was the stopping place for all the show people who were still playing the old Fisher Theater or the famous Schubert, the biggest houses in town. These theaters were vestiges of the great days of vaudeville, when playing a big theater in Detroit brought in almost as much money as in New York. George Burns and Gracie Allen had stayed at the Seville, as had Frank Sinatra, and Gilda grew up with these glittering names in the atmosphere.

Her father's dream became her dream as well. His nightmare also became hers.

"He had been having headaches for a couple of years. But really, there was no warning. He thought it was his glasses. It happened out of the clear blue. He suddenly developed brain cancer when I was twelve. One day—boom, it hit him. He went into the hospital for some routine tests, and really, as far as I was concerned, he never came out. At first, whenever he saw me, he would begin to cry. And then he just lay there like a vegetable for two years, terminally ill. His tumor was too far gone to remove. And then he died when I was fourteen years old," she said sadly, "and left a scrapbook of newspaper clippings. . . .

"He was the love of my life," Gilda said simply, sitting there at that big white table, with just a trace of a tear in her eye.

Gilda was away at summer camp the day he died. On August 10, 1960, in the early morning, she was sound asleep when the camp owner woke her up, saying her mother had called, her father had "taken a turn for the worse," and she should go home. She flew back to Detroit in a small plane. Her brother met her at the airport, and he did something he had never done before: he took her hand. Suddenly Gilda knew her father was dead.

In accord with the Jewish tradition, she sat shiva for a week, trying to pray for her father's soul, as relatives, friends, and well-wishers visited the house in an unending stream, all bringing food. After the week of shiva, still numb with shock, at her request Gilda returned to camp. She had rehearsed her part as Bloody Mary in the camp production of *South Pacific*, and she knew that her father would have said, "The show must go on!"

That same year, at age fourteen, Gilda first began to smoke.

When we got to know each other better, Gilda lamented that she had never had an appropriate mourning period for her father. Indeed, his death marked her whole family for the rest of their lives and, in Gilda's case, led to years of psychotherapy.

It was obvious that the fallout from her father's death had still not settled when I first met her that crisp autumn day five years afterward. You could tell from her posture, her body language, the vulnerable note in her voice: she was overwhelmed, frightened, and rudderless.

As if her father's death were not enough to strike the fear of God into Gilda, she had other cancer premonitions as well. Although unaware of all the specifics, Gilda knew that her family had an ominous history of the disease. Her grandmother had died of stomach cancer shortly before her birth. Her maternal aunt and two other relatives died of ovarian cancer, the same illness that eventually overwhelmed Gilda. Her mother had suffered from breast cancer but later recovered.

After he died Gilda studied every detail of her father's life and kept a voluminous file of news clippings about him.

Michael Moriarty, the actor, was amazed one day when, as he tells it:

"Gilda came up to me and said, 'My father knew your grandfather. Wait here, I'll get the clips.'

"And sure enough, she came back with clippings about the World Series between Detroit and the Chicago Cubs in 1935. My grandfather was a ballplayer and then a major-league umpire, and in one of the games he umpired he had thrown out several players and the manager—for slurs against Hank Greenberg, who was Jewish. My grandfather was fined for having done so, and Gilda's father and some other gentlemen raised a fund to pay his fine!"

This spirit of behind-the-scenes charity was a key motif in Gilda's life and one of her primary lifelines to the memory of her father.

Taking the cue from her father, Gilda hit on a unique, magical method of healing her wound and protecting herself from evil. She was avidly trying to build a bridge of humor across the huge abyss that had opened in her life. She was already an accomplished comedian, with a natural sense of timing and a quickness of mind that never failed to penetrate to the humorous essence of every issue, even ones she knew nothing whatever about.

Perhaps Gilda was somewhat better prepared for her final tragedy by her lifelong awareness of the power of the knowledge of death. It made her a philosopher, as well as a candidate for psychotherapy, from a very young age. When she underwent her childhood nightmare of cancer, the word was even more of a death sentence than it is today. Her world went out of control when her father died.

To Gilda, comedy was the only way a little girl could possibly regain power over the situation.

She saw comedy not only as a way to send and receive love, but also as a means of control. As she wrote:

". . . I always thought that my comedy grew from my neurotic way of life—the way that I would think *The plane is going to crash* before it took off, so then it wouldn't ever happen. I never leave the house without thinking the house will blow up or catch fire or whatever, because it's also like a magic way of making it not happen. . . ."

Even if she could not always control her life, Gilda knew very well how to control the artificial life of the theater. When she took the stage, she was well aware of her power as a fairy princess. She would let the audience laugh when she wanted them to laugh. And they would cry if she wanted them to cry.

One of her favorite characters was the tragic clown. She adored Charlie Chaplin. From her peculiarly constituted childhood, she had acquired a great love of vaudeville, circus, and magic as a way of convincing death the time was not yet at hand.

She definitely had a superstitious side. She had learned from her father to say "Bunny! Bunny!" on the first day of every month and really felt herself unlucky if she forgot to.

She sometimes tried to milk superstition for humor. We once did a vaudeville-style bit on the radio in Ann Arbor where she would say:

"You say you're not superstitious, but would you walk under a burning building? Would you light three cigarettes with the same ten-dollar bill? Would you take a chisel in your right hand and bring it sharply down on your left? And you claim you're not superstitious!"

Gilda's mother and brother had their own problems and

their own ways of dealing with the tragedy of Herman's death. Those ways did not always include Gilda.

The only other time Ellen or I can recall Henrietta and Mickey coming together to see Gilda in Ann Arbor was a day on which Gilda had suddenly become very serious, completely uncharacteristic for her. I asked her what was going on, and she got very tight-lipped, frowning her four-line frown with her piano-wire lips making a fifth line, like a stylized musical staff with a pair of snake eyes and a cute nose on F.

She began to chant:

"A trust. A trust. We're gonna bust a trust. We gotta bust a trust. There's a trust that we just gotta bust. . . ."

The trust, which Gilda came into when she turned twenty-one, was all part of the posthumous machinations of the real estate and hotel enterprise built by Herman Radner.

After Herman fell sick, the family had sold the Seville. After he died, they had bought another illustrious Detroit hotel, the Park Shelton, on Woodward and Kirby, which they had converted to an apartment residence. The Park Shelton, the jewel in the Radner crown, was located in the cultural center of Detroit, rather than along Hotel Row. It was not only a charming, classy joint; it was an extremely valuable piece of prime real estate, located just catty-corner from the Detroit Art Museum.

Gilda occasionally used to say, "I grew up in a hotel," even though she had never actually lived at either of the family's holdings. But she spent a great deal of time in them and always felt more at home in a hotel than nearly anywhere else.

The Radners sold the Park Shelton in 1967, when Gilda turned twenty-one. I was never able to learn whether or not she had successfully "busted the trust" a couple of years earlier, but in any case she came into a sizable inheritance when she came of age.

Even though we seldom saw Gilda's mother in Ann Arbor, Gilda often spoke of her. It was rarely in rapturous terms, but it was always masked with humor. She told stories that sounded so bizarre that they just might be true.

Henrietta was not consciously funny, according to Gilda, but she had what Gilda called "an infectious response" to humorous situations.

"My mother was feeling very low one day," Gilda told us many years after the fact.

"She was really playing the part of the sick, aging widow. It wasn't like her, really, because she always tried to keep herself active and pretty. Instead of a mastectomy, she would have a face-lift. That was a good attitude, but this was a bad time for her. I pleaded with her to go to the doctor, but she refused. She had prescribed for herself bed, fasting, and soap operas.

"I tried to help her out. But she refused to let anything be done for her.

" 'Can I get you a glass of water, at least?' I asked her.

" 'No. Don't bother,' she said, dramatically collapsing back onto her pillows.

"As she lay there, you could practically hear her stomach rumbling with hunger," Gilda said. "After a while she said:

" 'At least the people next door won't be able to smell cooking from my kitchen. They won't be able to come and cadge any nice, hot chicken soup like I used to make for you, darling!'

"When she mentioned her soup, she went into this reverie of mental tasting," Gilda said.

"Suddenly, there was a knock at the front door. My mother's eyes flew open. I went out to answer it. It was our next-door neighbor.

" 'My mother sent me,' the eight-year-old girl said as she stood on the threshold holding a large ceramic bowl.

" 'She wants to know if you have some soup she can borrow—any hot soup.'

" 'God help me!' my mother cried from the bedroom," Gilda said. "Her voice was suddenly back to its full power.

" 'Now the neighbors even smell my thoughts!' "

Gilda's mother had worked as a legal secretary, but inside she was also a frustrated performer like her husband. In her case the road not taken was ballet dancing. Toward her daughter she always took a complex attitude based on her own record of highs and lows: she insisted that Gilda should have been more beautiful, more helpful, less of a burden.

Gilda eventually took those qualities in her mother and made them screamingly funny, as in a savage "Saturday Night" sketch she did in which her mother, played by Jane Curtin, says:

"I begrudge you every breath you ever took!"

To others her mother's traits were screamingly otherwise.

"She was some kind of . . . of . . . *shopping creep*," Ellen Frank says of Gilda's mother. Ellen was one of Gilda's closest friends, having known her since fifth grade, and she knew Mrs. Radner very well.

"Henrietta was a spoiled, pampered Jewish princess, a real bitch. She and Gilda had no relation at all.

"Even today, her son, Michael, comes home from work at two P.M. to drive Henrietta to shopping malls! How that girl ever came out of that family, I'll never know," Ellen adds.

In her book Gilda mentions that her mother came to visit

her only once while she was sick. In spite of their continual friction, Gilda later tried to write of Henrietta with kindness. Even though Gilda considered her petty and willful, she still loved her mother in her own way.

Henrietta had been quite beautiful as a young woman. Inside, Gilda always compared herself unfavorably with her. That led Gilda to strive very hard so her mother and father would both have been proud. According to her dancing teacher, Gilda always worked like a demon at dancing simply because she wanted to dance as well as Henrietta had. It is hard to say if she was trying to show her up. This was not Gilda's way. But she always worked hard at what she liked and was a perfectionist when it came to performing.

In college Gilda had not yet totally transmuted this psychodrama into dancing and performing. She became more openly hostile toward Henrietta. She rarely spoke to her or about her without a trace of a sneer or a catch in her voice. She liked to make her mother the butt of her jokes.

Gilda's motherward affections always went out to Dibby, her childhood nanny, whom she spoke of fondly, warmly, and frequently.

"You've heard me speak of Dibby?!"

That was one of her favorite lines, delivered with a rising inflection and just a touch of a "cultured" accent, and it always got a laugh because we had heard her speak of Dibby so often. Gilda telephoned Dibby once a week or so, and they corresponded as well.

For many years, even until the end, Dibby was Gilda's alter ego, her sounding board, her bulwark, and the original source of much of her comedy. Dibby, whose real name was Mrs. Elizabeth Clementine Gillies, had been widowed in World War I. She reared three children of her own, then lived on a small farm in Ontario by herself until she came to work for Gilda's family when Gilda was four months old.

Dibby originally came into Gilda's life on a whim. She had been in Detroit visiting relatives when she noticed an ad Gilda's parents had put in the paper for a temporary housekeeper. Dibby wanted some extra money and thought she'd try it for two weeks. She went upstairs to see the baby, Gilda, and she fell in love when Gilda turned right over and gave her a big smile. The Radners hired her on the spot, and she ended up staying for eighteen years. She got the name Dibby because baby Gilda could not pronounce "Mrs. Gillies." She called her "Mita Dibby" instead, then just plain Dibby.

Dibby was a delightfully warm woman, the apple-pie mom of everyone's dreams, and only she gave the sympathy Gilda desperately needed at that time.

Dibby and Gilda were inseparable during Gilda's school days. Unlike Henrietta, Dibby instantly accepted Gilda for what she was and did not try to change her. This was especially true of Gilda's body, which in those days was, it must be said, a chubby one. When Gilda came home crying because someone at school had called her fat, Dibby gave her something that later became her main prescription for humor. She said:

"Say you're fat before they can. Let them know that you *are* fat and you don't care. If they say you are, just make a joke about it and laugh. Just *you* tell *them* before they get to it."

That was how Gilda got through her tubby and tormented teens, using humor to cope with her life.

"Humor," she declared, "is just truth, only faster!"

Dibby, who was hard of hearing and, as Gilda said, cute as a button, was the inspiration for Gilda's great "Saturday Night" character Emily Litella, the spunky but somewhat deaf editorial-replier on "Weekend Update." "Never mind," Emily's famous tag line, was Dibby's favorite and most characteristic expression. Dibby often gave Gilda hilarious suggestions for Emily bits, and Gilda would frequently ask "Saturday Night" writers to talk to Dibby on the phone so they could catch the flavor of her expressions and the subtlety of her wit.

In the acknowledgments to her first book, *Roseanne Roseannadanna's "Hey, Get Back to Work!" Book*, Gilda refers to Mom as "Mrs. H. Radner." Dibby gets two acknowledgments, under "Dibby" and "Elizabeth Clementine Gillies."

In Dibby's later years she was frequently in and out of the hospital. Already an international star, Gilda often went to visit her. Dibby told Gilda that after every time she visited, the nurses treated her one hundred percent better.

Her spirit remained indomitable:

"I can't hear and I can't see and I can't walk, but other than that I'm fine," she told Gilda in one of their last conversations.

Shortly after Gilda died, Dibby also passed away, at age ninety-seven.

Because of her hostility toward her mother, Gilda always went to her friend Judy Glucklich's house on weekends, when so many of the Detroit kids went home.

Suzan Smith, Judy's cousin, recalls:

"I always thought Gilda was a member of our family, she was at Judy's house so often. I always used to call her my cousin, and I really thought she *was* my cousin, from the Glucklich side of the family. It wasn't until I knew Gilda as a grown-up that I learned we were *not* related and that she used to go over there so she could avoid spending the weekend with her mother!"

As for Mickey, Gilda loved him, but . . . as he himself has put it:

"It took me only a few years to go from being my father's son to my sister's brother!"

Mickey has made a career out of successfully managing the considerable Radner assets. But, at least in Gilda's mind, he seemed to have never grown up. About his love life, Gilda always used to laugh. She would occasionally try to fix him up with someone, but, according to her, it always ended in disaster.

"He'll never get married until my mother dies," she'd say resignedly, with a shake of the head. As of this writing, Henrietta is eighty-six years old and going strong. Mickey is still unmarried.

To those of us who were close to her in those days, it was always clear that the driving force of Gilda's humor was her need and capacity for love. For much of her life she had been the poor little rich girl, whose astounding capacity for kindness made everyone she met fall in love with her.

Because of Gilda's irregular and painful childhood, she reached out to her friends to make them her family. And so it was around the same white table, in that marvelous, sunny kitchen in that magically turreted house in Ann Arbor that Gilda and the rest of us became blood brothers and sisters, partners in diets and crime, undergoing together our first fasts, first pigouts, and first experiments in being unkind to our bodies.

There was such a quality of loving and sharing and community that Haven Street remained with all of us as the golden summer of young adulthood. Even casual visitors to that enchanted turret remember the special vibrations, not to be found anywhere else in the known world of that time.

We still thought of ourselves as "kids" then and for many

more years afterward. Perhaps ours was the last generation that luxuriated in a pleasant adolescence, gently inclining into a much more painful "Boomer" adulthood.

During this university period Gilda loved to perform, philosophize, debate, and discuss.

"Haven Street was Gilda's stage," as Ellen Frank recalls it. "And also her refuge. She had a deep need to be the center of attention. But at the same time she also needed her privacy."

She loved literature and poetry and still liked to read Charles Dickens and Emily Dickinson, whom she had discovered in high school. We would hold marathon discussions on life and death, always punctuated with recitations of loud poetry and bursts of wild humor. And food was never far out of the picture.

Once, for instance, Ellen made the most delicious rice pudding of all time. It was great, made with cinnamon and brown sugar and little tiny pieces of lemon peel. Wow! I can still taste it.

We all ate liberally of it at dinner while discussing some abstruse theme—whether God existed, or whether you could ever do anything original, or whether people *fuck* anymore.

Anyway, later that night, as we all prepared to sleep in the huge bedroom off the turret, Gilda, wearing her pink nightgown, said:

"Dave! Dave!"

"What?"

"I just got the greatest thought! I can't believe it! This is so great!"

"What is it?"

"No, this is incredible! This is really a remarkable, amazing thought!"

"Gilda, what *is* it? You're making me crazy!"

"Listen. Listen. Bring me the rest of the rice pudding, and I'll tell you."

"OK."

So I got out of bed and went into the kitchen, got the rice pudding, got a fork, and brought it all to her in the bedroom.

Without any hurry whatsoever she ate, enjoying every delicious bite until the whole bowl was empty.

Meanwhile, Elena and I were becoming more and more agitated.

"Gilda," I said, "if you don't tell us your fabulous thought, I won't be able to sleep!"

"The thought," said Gilda, "was this:

" 'Never go to sleep without eating the rest of the great rice pudding Ellen made!' "

We fell over on our backs with laughter. We were Gilda's captive audience.

In those days, Gilda and I regularly stood in front of the bathroom or bedroom mirror, doing comedy bits and parodies of commercials. One of her most memorable was an ad for her particular brand of tampons. She would manhandle a tampon every which way, then, with her dazzling, depraved smile, deliver her tag line directly into the mirror:

"Up yours!"

At that time, knowing what a fantastic wit she was, I gave Gilda her first job in show business.

I was able to do so because by 1965 I was already a big shot at the campus radio station, WCBN.

Gilda quickly distinguished herself as a "weather girl" on the WCBN News. She then began appearing as a regular on my morning show, "The Saltman-Segal Psychedelicatessen," cohosted by Steve Segal. Steve went on to become a famous radio disc jockey in Boston and Los Angeles under the sobriquet "the Obscene Steven Clean."

Gilda was sensational in her job as a weather girl, though highly irregular. For instance, she liked to imitate a radio with static, giving the weather as:

"Grrr cloudybzzz.

"Periods of ssssssrain followedgrrr by bssssun.

"Bip-pip-pip snowstorm znrr."

On the morning program, she would sit in the announce booth, making faces at Steve and me, who were sitting at a master control console opposite. In that announce booth she improvised the first tap dance ever broadcast over the radio. She would occasionally play an august personage known as Lady Bucket, who was sort of a cross between Emily Litella and Lady Douchebag from one of Gilda's sketches of the "Saturday Night" era.

She was fond of wordplay at this time and used to get great pleasure from imaginary conversations with her husband, Lord Bucket.

"Bucket, I *can*!" she would exclaim in a stentorian yet matronly tenor, sounding just like a character out of Dickens.

Gilda and I both loved to listen to comedy records in college. Her favorites were Mel Brooks and Carl Reiner's *The Two Thousand Year Old Man* and anything by Stan Freberg. She was very impressed by Freberg's novelty single, "John and Marsha," presumably intrigued by his ability to create a hilarious comic effect by just having the actors repeat the same two words, *John* and *Marsha*, in differing tones of voice.

It was in these days that I began to call Gilda "Gillis" or

"Gillies," nicknames she liked because they had called her "Gillis" at summer camp and Dibby's last name was Gillies. Her parents had named her Gilda because they were watching that old Rita Hayworth movie the night she was conceived. (Thank God they weren't watching *Hellzapoppin.*) *Gilda* is an ancient English name, completely inappropriate for a Jewess except that it means "golden" or "covered with gold."

Once, in some college literature anthology, we found an old Scottish poem about someone named "Gillie," and even though we could not exactly figure out what it meant, we loved to recite it in loud voices to each other, one line at a time. We memorized it because we both had the impression that it described "Gillis" to a T.

Here's the only bit of it I remember, since I cannot seem to find it preserved anywhere:

Of all their maidens mild as meid
  Was nane sae gymp as Gillie;
As ony rose her rude was reid,
  Her lire was like the lily.
Bot zallow, zallow was hir heid,
  And sche of luif sae sillie,
Thof a' hir kin suld hae bein deid,
  Sche wuld hae bot sweit Willie.

If you read it out loud, the words suddenly begin to make sense, and you realize it is an excellent thumbnail sketch of a charmer who was ready to throw it all away for love.

From early on Gilda used to love playing the wag on the radio, as in the following sketch we did on WCBN. It was not entirely original, but we knew even then that to be original in this world is not easy:

GILDA: Did you ever stop to think how little we go to school in a year?
STEVE: What do you mean? I work like a horse. I even wear a harness to class.
GILDA: Horse duty. You don't go to school at all. Even in Leap Year! Set up the blackboard, I'll show you.

(Here we had sound effects of a blackboard moving into place.)

GILDA: OK, now in Leap Year there are 366 days. Put that down, 366.

(Sound effect of chalk on blackboard)

Now, you sleep eight hours a day. That is one-third of the day, 24 hours, that you sleep. So you sleep one-third of the year, or 122 days. That gives you 244 days left.

(More sound of chalk writing)

Now, another eight hours of the day you have for rest and recreation. So that's another 122 days you don't go to school. Which leaves you 122 days remaining. Of these 122 days, you don't go to school on Sundays. There are 52 weeks in a year, so 52 Sundays from 122 leaves you 70 days. You get half a day off every Saturday. Half of 52 is 26; subtract from 70, and it leaves you 44. Dave, how long do you take for lunch every day?
DAVE: About an hour, hour and a half.

GILDA: An hour and a half. So in one week you spend more than half a day eating. That makes about 28 days a year you do nothing but sit around and eat—especially you, Dave. Twenty-eight days from 44—that leaves you 16 days. Every year you get at least two weeks' vacation, even if you take summer school. That's 14 days from 16. That leaves you only two days. Those two days are the Fourth of July and Labor Day. Take those two days off! They're holidays! Ya gotta be nuts to go to class on a holiday! So you see—you don't go to school even one day in the year!

That sketch was perhaps truer of Gilda than anyone else at the University of Michigan.

"I never quite knew what Gilda was doing in college," recalls one of her old college friends. "Only rarely did I see her reading or cramming for an exam. When I saw her at the apartment, she was usually joking around with a visitor like me."

In fact, Gilda got through college by spending a great deal of time in the dean's office convincing him she was under too much pressure academically. Instead of classes she devoted her time to the theater.

She had comic roles in the University of Michigan and Ann Arbor Civic Theater productions of *The Magic Horn*, *Lysistrata*, and *Hotel Paradiso*. She played Morgan le Fay in *Camelot* and lead roles in *The Taming of the Shrew* and *She Stoops to Conquer*. As she began to make a name for herself in Ann Arbor, Gilda really thought she would stay there forever as an eternal undergraduate.

Even though she was doing well in the theater, she did not seriously consider show business as a career. She regarded it as fantastic and deluded that you could actually make money playing the same games you played with your friends or with collegiate audiences. She had a half-cooked notion that she would eventually enter one of the helping professions, perhaps as a teacher of retarded children, who, like her former fat self, were sure to be beautiful on the inside, even if apparently deformed on the outside. She had even worked with such kids while in high school. Her failure to graduate from the university put the kibosh on this plan, however, and gave the theater a nonpareil performer.

Another thing Gilda was doing in those days was eating and then going on ridiculous diets. For Gilda, Haven Street was a benchmark in a lifelong series of disastrous diets. She was a compulsive eater and a compulsive dieter, obsessed with her childhood fear of being fat. Only another fat kid can understand this. She sometimes used to stand in front of the mirror and cry.

Gilda continually tried to make her fear of fat into humor, as Dibby had advised. Once when she was already a "Saturday Night" star, she arranged a number of her childhood photos on a bulletin board and headed them "Memories of Fatness, by Gilda Radner." Each photo of herself as an indubitably chubby mite had a caption: "Fat," or "Hello, I'm fat," or, sitting on a horse as a cowgirl, "Howdy, I'm fat." One of them read, "Very fat," and indeed between ages ten and fifteen she was.

During the first years of "Saturday Night," when asked how she got so funny, she would always reply: "It's because I was so fat."

Indeed, even when she weighed a scant 110, with her bones sticking out, she would say:

"I am still a fat person, really. What my body looks like

now is pure vanity. My psychology is still the same as that fat girl I grew up as. That's why I'm not afraid to do anything comedically. I'll walk into a wall. I'm not afraid of anything. I don't worry about femininity—I think I am feminine. But I know I've scared many men off because of humor. I'll be funny instead of feminine. You're not likely to see me sitting back at a party being pretty."

When she would return to Detroit for a visit with her mother and brother, her favorite nighttime activity was to put on one of her mother's old nightgowns and scour the cupboards and refrigerator for food.

It was not only being the fattest and "getting scapegoated," as she used to put it, that stripped her of vanity and provided the negative reinforcement and deprivation that led to her painfully true brand of humor. To that you had to add the positive reinforcement she received in her family for being funny.

Humor was one of the only ways she could get to her mother, to make her laugh if she was angry or not paying attention—which was frequently.

Gilda used to tell about her brother and herself eating dinner at the kitchen table. Her mother would command:

" 'Don't talk at the table. It gives you indigestion.'

"So we'd start singing under our breath, you know, some awful song. It always made my mother gnash her teeth, but my father would laugh, and then my mother would finally have to laugh in spite of herself."

By her sixteenth birthday Gilda finally had dropped a good deal of weight. She was proud enough to allow herself to be photographed in a bathing suit, standing on top of her brother's motorcycle in the large backyard of her twenties Tudor home on Wildemere Street in the Palmer Park section of northwest Detroit.

By the time Gilda graduated from Liggett School, her

high school in Detroit, a thin person inside had struggled out. From then on she carried her fatness in her mind, but to her it seemed to hover around her body like a wraith. She was still a sucker for every diet in the world.

For our university-level diet instruction, we had to thank the charming and devilish Bill Ayers, just a quiet guy from a wealthy family in Chicago who shook up this country in a major way when he eventually became leader of the infamous Weathermen.

In college he was a very sweet, highly intelligent fellow who had read somewhere that only by eating lots of gluten bread can you possibly hope to lose weight and be healthy.

Because he had a healthy interest in Gilda and a desire to be present at as many of our excellent Elena and Ellen dinners as possible, Bill found it necessary to convince us that we must eat exactly as he outlined and that he had better supervise us personally if we were really to have any chance at all of losing weight. None of us had ever even heard of gluten bread before. But he put it in such a charming way that we bought it.

Gilda in those days had one truly unique, even mysterious, dietary habit that occasionally took place exactly half an hour after dinner. She called it "making up a meal for my mother."

To do this in what she considered an honorable manner, she always made sure she ate, or at least intended to eat, small amounts of Jewish food every day.

I don't know how the timing worked. That was the mysterious part. But when the phone rang half an hour after dinner, Gilda would on these occasions say:

"Wait a minute. It's my mother, and I have to make up a meal for her."

She would concentrate for about six rings and then:

"Hello, Mom? I knew it was you."

She was always right.

"Oh, great," Gilda would continue. "Oh, do you *have* to know? Well, I'm having chicken soup with matzo balls. . . ."

She would describe a meal she either had eaten or was going to eat, depicting it in a certain special kind of progressive subjunctive mood that made one unclear about the exact timing.

The meal she made up invariably seemed to contain large quantities of Jewish food and small amounts of gluten bread. But she told it in such a way that she never really lied to her mother.

The aforementioned Bill Ayers became one of America's most wanted. Ellen Frank recalls that he convinced her to sleep with him to prove she was politically correct. Then Ellen took up with his brother Ricky. Ricky and Ellen split up, and Ricky and Gilda became lovers. According to Ellen, Gilda helped Ricky escape the military draft by financing his trip to Canada, since he was cut off from his own family fortune because of his political views. Like many American draft protesters, he remained in Canada during the entire Vietnam War.

Years later, when they were no longer deeply underground, Bill Ayers and his wife, the equally notorious and equally sweet Bernardine Dohrn, came to New York because they wanted to see Gilda in *Lunch Hour*, the play she was doing with Sam Waterston.

In this play Gilda enjoyed the fact that she got to use her own enormous quilted mauve Pierre Deux purse onstage as a prop. If you were sitting close enough, you could get a whiff of the jumbo twelve-packs of bubble gum and cartons of Benson & Hedges Longs she always carried inside.

"I like a really big purse, and I mean *really* big," she commented once on the subject of her bag-ladyness. "I always like to take a little of home with me wherever I go.

People laugh at me, but they're the same ones that always need a toenail clipper or a big steel file that they end up borrowing from me."

Bill called Gilda to arrange tickets, which she did. Then, after they went backstage to see her, they had a nice chat and went out to eat. An underground legend has sprung up over this meeting, in which Gilda's giant purse figures prominently.

In the legend, Bill and Bernardine were still underground when they made this visit to New York. The legend avers that they were in disguise, and that backstage Gilda rummaged through the oral pacifiers and manicure tools in her voluminous purse to give the fugitives a great deal of money, with which they continued hiding out.

A simple comparison of dates puts the lie to this story, which has been told and retold. It is easy to understand how this story gained currency, however, since Gilda was always generous with money and because the detail of her purse made it sound convincing to those who knew her well.

Many of our endless procession of Haven Street dinner-and-diet guests have since become eminent in their fields, by hook or by crook. We also hosted Bill Kirchen, the funkabilly rock star of Commander Cody and His Lost Planet Airmen; Steve Segal, the aforementioned radio star; Harvey Wasserman, the political activist and historian; Roger Rapoport, the journalist; and many others.

Around that kitchen table we debated the central issues of the sixties: Vietnam, drugs, rock and roll, sex, and gluten bread.

Theme dinners were one of Ellen's contributions to the Haven Street ambience. Once she made an Indonesian *rijsttafel* using a recipe she had obtained from one of her far-flung network of international friends. There were so many courses and so many guests we had to abandon the kitchen table. I went to a lumberyard and procured a huge wooden door along with some cinder blocks. We made a giant table out of the door and served dinner in the living room. Gilda and Ellen used the occasion to scope out potential boyfriends among the dozens of dinner guests, who seemed to show up from all over town, invited or not.

The dinner created such a stir in Ann Arbor that even the next day some people we barely knew appeared, expecting to be fed, claiming to be "friends of the guy who gave you the recipe."

Ellen and Elena had managed to make a tasty soup out of the leftovers, which, with good grace, they fed to these upstarts.

Finally, the last straw: someone knocked on the door and said he had heard about the great dinner and claimed to be "a friend of a friend of the guy who gave you the recipe."

We were dumbstruck at his audacity. The soup was gone. But Gilda rose to the occasion. She went into the kitchen and put some warm water into a bowl. She added a little curry powder to it and handed it to the visitor, saying:

"OK, this is the soup of the soup we made out of the *rijsttafel*."

One of the high-water marks of our tenure at Haven Street was the night the bat got in.

This is one of those stories better acted out than written, and after she had recovered from the shock, Gilda always loved to act it out because to provide verisimilitude she got to shake brooms in the air and march around the room swinging, swatting, and shrieking like a Jericho trumpet.

But at the time it actually took place she found it anything but funny.

It happened the night Gilda decided to sleep in the turret. Normally the turret was Ellen's turf, but we were all intrigued by the idea of sleeping there, so occasionally Ellen would relinquish her bed and allow someone else to enjoy the pleasure of nodding out in a gothic novel.

That unforgettable night, Gilda said she wanted to sleep in thc turret because, sleeping in the large bedroom with the rest of us, she couldn't hear herself think. So we helped her put her sheets and pillows onto Ellen's bed, which was simply a thick mattress thrown on the floor in the manner of students everywhere.

Even though Gilda had closed the door to the turret, we could hear muffled sounds as she adjusted everything just right for herself, pulling the bed a little over here, pushing the table a little over there, until presumably everything was all cozy-snuggly-warmy-warm.

We all dozed. Around midnight, we were all sound asleep.

The next thing I remember is hearing a tremendous crash and a loud scream coming from the turret. I woke up halfway and peered groggily into the darkness. Suddenly the door to the turret flew open, and out ran Gilda in her nightgown, as if she were pursued by all the hounds of hell.

"Help! Help! Wake up!" she shouted.

Elena and Ellen woke up right away and turned on all the lights. But I was still slow to arouse. When my eyes finally opened all the way, it was to a horrifying sight: a giant bat came flying out of the turret at full speed, passing directly over my head, apparently in hot pursuit of Gilda.

Ellen and Elena were wide awake by now and both

shrieking at the top of their lungs. Gilda was running in figure eights through the apartment, screaming:

"My hair! My hair! It's going for my hair!"

Putting my hand on top of my head, I rolled out of bed and ran for the broom closet. Ellen, showing great presence of mind, went for yesterday's newspaper.

I pulled out two brooms, a mop, and a feather duster and passed out an item to each of us. Ellen rapidly improvised four hats made out of newspaper, which she issued in double-quick fashion.

"Put this on your head," she instructed.

Gilda grabbed one and said, in an authoritative, if frightened, voice:

"Right, they go for your hair. They get their little claws in your hair, and you can never get them out. Yuck!"

It sounded bad, so we all put the newspaper hats on our heads.

Brandishing a broom as if it were a bayonet, I asked, in a voice ready for battle, "Where's the bat?"

The bat indeed had disappeared. We knew no windows were open. So we quickly deduced the darkling intruder must still be somewhere on the premises.

Pulling the paper cones well over our ears, we quickly deployed the brooms and organized a patrol of the apartment.

"You stay in front, Dave, because you're the guy," Gilda said.

With me in the lead, brandishing my broom, Elena and Ellen protecting our flanks, and Gilda bringing up the rear walking backward with her mop waving out to stern, we slinked around the apartment crouching and stepping gingerly, like the Beagle Boys en route to Scrooge McDuck's money bin.

"Hah!" I shouted, thrusting the broom into the space

behind the kitchen door. Nothing. The girls were all following me, sticking so close I could barely move. After I shouted, they all thrust their weapons simultaneously, and answered, like a chorus:

"Hah!"

We could not find the bat. After ten minutes of careful searching, all of us jabbing our weapons into various recesses, I straightened up and said, "Maybe it flew out the same way it got in?"

The girls did not really believe this, but it made them relax a little bit. They straightened up too. Suddenly, we all got a good look at one another, sophisticated college students in our pajamas with paper cones on our heads and dirty brooms, mop, and feather duster held in the port arms position.

We began to laugh.

Just as we commenced laughing, the bat swooped over our heads. We could see its little black ratlike face and its sharp greenish claws, which did indeed seem pointed at our hair. The air shook with the beat of its huge wings and the counterwave of two brooms, a mop, and a feather duster whooshing through space. Swat! Swat! Swat! Swish! Our weapons tried to find the mark. But that little sucker was fast! We missed him entirely.

The bat proceeded to do what I believe stunt flyers call an Immelmann: a figure eight in the air, reversing direction instantly and buzzing us again.

Again we beat our brooms in vain. I had an idea.

"The window," I said, ducking as the bat again turned on a dime and homed in on us once more. "On three. One. Two. Three!"

Stooping as low as we could, we all ran to the living room window. The girls protected the rear by swishing their brooms as I quickly unfastened the catch.

The window opened, we looked around. The bat had vanished again.

We began to search, brooms at the ready, hats on our heads. Suddenly, Elena spotted the bat:

"There he is!" She pointed at the curtains on the other side of the room. Sure enough, the bat was hanging upside down from the curtain rod. Slowly we walked, step by step, inch by inch, until we were within sweeping distance.

I held up my hand. One finger. Two fingers. Three fingers.

Swish! Swish! Swat!

We swung for the bleachers, and the bat took off like, well, like a bat off a rod. But he took evasive action and somehow got us turned back-to-front, swatting at cross-purposes. As Gilda lunged for the bat, Ellen's broom landed squarely in her face with a resounding "Smack!"

Gilda shrieked: "Aaarrrggghhhh! He got on my face! He's in my hair! Aaaiiiiieeeeekkk!"

The bat must have gotten a good laugh out of that because, without further ado, he made a beeline (or is that a batline?) for the open window and flew out into the night.

Slamming the window behind him, we tore the cones off our heads and inspected Gilda's face and hair and then our own. Whatever bats leave in your hair, none of us appeared to have any of it. Gilda's face sported a reddish broom-sized welt. Ellen apologized for swatting her. Slowly, we breathed a collective sigh.

Gilda looked at Ellen and then at the rest of us. In a relieved but slightly shaking voice she said:

"I don't think I wanna hear myself think anymore. Ell, you can have the turret back. I'm sleeping in my own bed from now on!"

Gilda always described herself as "not political." She

never attended a demonstration or any of the "teach-ins" Ann Arbor was so proud of and so famous for.

"I felt guilty when I saw people becoming more politically active," she said about this time in her life, "but I felt good doing my theater work and radio work and children's workshops. Somehow, the movement never moved me."

Gilda was well liked in college, but she impressed many people as kooky, out of touch with the serious atmosphere that hung like a backdrop over Ann Arbor in the mid-sixties. She was definitely "anti-intellectual" in the sense that, while she appreciated real intellect and in actual smarts could have given points and spades to anyone on campus, she found the university atmosphere false and full of inflated gasbags.

Nevertheless, throughout her years in Ann Arbor Gilda was observing everything that was going on and sharpening her beak on it. She always loved to use politics and current events for material, letting her developing characters, who were just various facets of her own self, take off on it.

While we were in school, for instance, in the mid-1960s, the Detroit riots took place. Gangs of enraged blacks burned down sections of the city that are still not built back up today.

Sitting in that sunny white kitchen thirty-eight miles away, around a table full of gluten bread and unsalted butter and leftover *rijsttafel*, Bill Ayers, Ellen, Elena, and I took this very seriously and debated various political positions on civil rights. But Gilda made it into a joke that even more tellingly revealed everyone's true inner feelings.

As happens with many fiery political debates, a sudden, uncomfortable pause occurred as the debaters refueled and rearmed. Gilda stepped right in with the only thing she had said in an hour and a half:

"Well, I am not political, but the last time I was in Detroit," she said, "I made one of those gangs run like hell!"

We all stared.

"You did? How?" Bill asked.

"It was easy. I just stuck out my tongue and ran—and they ran after me!"

One of Gilda's stock comedy items in those days was an imitation of the poses in a men's muscle magazine that someone had left at the apartment. It never failed to make everyone collapse with laughter. Gilda would flex her arms, puff up her chest, and, in the manner of a wrestling announcer, make up names that sounded like musclemen:

"Dave DELtoid."

"Arnold SCHNOTZenwasser."

"Big Ric BLATZ."

Each name would be accompanied by a different pose. Maybe you had to be there, but believe me, there was nothing funnier than seeing the slenderizing, feminine Jewish princess transforming her lithe body from a front curl to a back triceps to a double biceps posture, announcing those absurd names in a loudspeakerlike warble.

She also delivered some excellent semicomic versions of fifties and sixties rock tunes, foreshadowing Candy Slice and Rhonda Weiss of the "Saturday Night" days. She said she liked records best in the fifties because you did not have to buy the whole album—you could just buy the 45. Her special favorite was Lou Christie's mid-sixties hit "Lightnin' Strikes," which she did with a jump that made you think there was broken glass behind her.

In those days, smoking dope was a most underground, bohemian activity, the ultimate in depravity in the common mind. Along with Communists, no persons were considered more marginal, more dangerous, than "dope addicts." Smoking was done behind locked doors and drawn curtains. We never imagined the day would come when Ann Arbor would declare marijuana possession to be no more serious than a parking ticket. And after that happened we never could have imagined it would revert back to the old way of "Reefer Madness" and that even we ourselves would eventually tremble with fear when we heard that someone was an "addict" or, worse, "junkie."

In any case, it was in that house on Haven that Gilda and her friends all first fulfilled Bob Dylan's commandment that "everybody must get stoned." All tended to undergo fits of the "blind munchies" after intoxication. That was, for Gilda, a discovery of the notion that you "eat to come down," eat to change your inner state in some way. It was an evil discovery that dogged her until the end of her life.

Gilda rarely drank and was never a hard-core druggie, although when she became a star she usually kept marijuana in her house for her friends and once went through a short period when she enjoyed her vodka. She smoked grass occasionally, but she did not like herself high because she either laughed uncontrollably or got very introspective and became as quiet as a mouse. After fifteen minutes of either she could not stand it anymore and almost always tried to come down right away, by eating. Food was always her addictive substance of choice.

4

Cowgirl of Camp Tamakwa

"The fat girl took so long"

GILDA'S CHILDHOOD PROMINENTLY FEATURED THAT AWKWARD painfulness that when looked at through the lens of her humor always seemed hilariously funny. It was the Judy Miller show, with spin-offs.

To Gilda, Judy Miller *was* her childhood self. For the most part, the Gilda you saw on "Saturday Night" was the real Gilda.

"It's not something that divides in my life, that suddenly I start acting funny, you know," Gilda once told an interviewer. Her whole secret, all the more hidden for its perfect obviousness, was that she made her life into her art. She once told *Rolling Stone*:

"When I'm doing Judy Miller, it's amazing how my mind clears away. I have to just completely forget about whether people are looking up my skirt, and just flop around and be five.

"My best girlfriend, Judy, who now lives in Toronto, once said to me, 'Boy, Gilda, it's real strange to see you making a living at what you did in my bedroom the whole time we were growing up!' "

In second grade, Gilda made her show business debut. She was a little disappointed that it was not on her favorite TV show, "Milky's Movie Party," starring Milky the Clown. But it was on another Detroit kid's show, "Sagebrush Shorty," that she got her first taste of the highs and heartbreaks of the limelight.

"My dad got us on this show, and all these kids at Hampton Elementary School called me up who had never spoken to me before and wanted me to say hello. I thought, Oh, I'm going to have so many friends. We watched cartoons, and they fed us ice cream and potato chips. I was real fat and had on a crinoline dress. The stage manager kept trying to get me to put my legs together because you could see my panties. When we got to the part where you can say hello to people, I read my list of thirty-five names. I remember the stage manager saying to Shorty, 'The other kids can't say anything because the fat girl took so long!' "

Shortly after this episode, under Dibby's guidance, Gilda consciously and deliberately became funny. It happened the day a neighbor kid named Mark taunted her:

"Hey, I saw you outside in your underwear!"

"You did not!" Gilda countered indignantly.

"Did!"

"Did *not*!" She ran into the house, crying hysterically. She thought to herself, What happened? Did I like go insane for a minute and really go outside in my underwear? Could Mark have happened to be riding his bike right at that same time and seen me on the front porch?

Right then and there, at eight years old, Gilda made a pact with herself. Dibby was right. No one was ever going to catch her off guard like that again. Mark had made her feel out of control, and she wanted to be in control. So half an hour after her humiliation she put on a bathing suit and put her underwear on over it, and very deliberately, when Mark was out in his front yard, she went onto her own front porch and, twirling around like an underwear model, yelled loud enough for everyone to hear:

"Hey, everybody! I am outside here in my underwear!"

When recalling this years later, she laughed: "I found that I could defuse whatever people might say about my being fat by joking about it first. That way they would have to deal with me as a person. If you can *decide* to be funny, I decided it then. I knew I wasn't going to make it on looks."

At eight years old, Gilda first went to Camp Maplehurst, in rural Michigan.

At nine, at camp, she first met Pam Katz, who became her lifelong friend. By coincidence, Pam became a psychotherapist specializing in cancer cases. She was one of Gilda's rocks during her illness. During that awful period, Gilda found solace in a support group in California called the Wellness Community. She describes it in loving detail in her book. Pam is now setting up a Wellness Community in Boston, as Gilda asked her to do the year she died.

"I've got the legacy," Pam said. "This is the only thing she ever asked me to do in her life. I've got to do it."

When Gilda was ten years old, in Detroit, she had her first official brush with fame. She sat in the backseat of their car as her father drove her out to the golf course.

"I felt so safe," she said, "and like such a celebrity."

She loved to sit in the backseat like this when her father drove her to school every day, because it made her feel as if she was someone terribly important and he was her chauffeur.

On the golf course her father introduced her to Milton

Berle, who had been a guest at the Seville. She shook his hand.

"For once, he didn't tell any 'big putz' jokes." Gilda laughed as she remembered this years later, on the disastrous night Uncle Miltie hosted "Saturday Night Live."

The same year Gilda met Milton Berle, she asked her parents if she could leave the public schools and attend private school. She was influenced in this by a girl who lived across the street. The neighbor liked very much going to the Liggett School for Girls, a private academy then located in the Indian Village district on the east side of Detroit, near the river. As Gilda approached her parents with this revolutionary idea, she tried to be very adult, as only ten-year-old girls can be. She negotiated with her parents like their little gonif, convincing them that only at Liggett could she get the good education that was her birthright. She was amazed when her parents agreed.

One reason they agreed was that the Radners were already planning to end a routine they had fallen into, and had thrown Gilda and her brother into, for the previous ten years.

Henrietta could not take the winters in Michigan. So they always spent the four winter months in Florida, with Herman shuttling back and forth to take care of his business interests in Detroit. It had worked all right, from Henrietta's perspective anyway, for the first ten years of Gilda's life. Gilda and Mickey would start school in Detroit in September, then in November her parents would take them out and enroll them in a school in Florida, where they would go until the middle of March. In March they would return to Detroit, where Gilda would finish her school until the summer. As a result of this migratory education, neither she nor her brother had any friends either in Detroit *or* in Florida.

Gilda used to tell us how she would wait behind the door of the Detroit classroom in March. All the kids had been classmates, playmates, and friends the whole year. She was convinced they were very excited that a new girl was coming. But she felt they were disappointed when they found out it would just be Gilda, "the same old girl from September." So Gilda was crushed the same way year after year.

Because of this seminomadic way of life, Gilda never knew whom to invite to her birthday parties, except relatives. Her birthday was in the summer, the Detroit end of the year, and she did not have any school friends close enough to ask.

In Florida one year she made friends with a girl from her class and invited her over to dinner. During dinner Gilda threw a temper tantrum about something or other. The next day, in school, they had "show and tell," and this girl told the whole class how she had gone to Gilda's house and had watched her have a tantrum at dinner. Gilda wanted to crawl into a hole and die.

Instead of crawling, however, Gilda began to eat. Perhaps she was trying to insulate herself from people by building a wall of fat around her heart. Or perhaps she ate because it was a life-affirming act. In any case, her brother did the same. She has said that at this time they both looked like "balloon children, no-necked monsters."

The one constant in her later childhood life became her new summer camp, Camp Tamakwa, in the middle of the lake country of Algonquin Provincial Park, Ontario. She always remembered her camp days with fondness even though she suffered there too.

Because Gilda was chubby, she always got the bad parts in the girls' games, like playing the servant of the beautiful princess. She did not know how to get out of this pickle, and she would stay up half the night worrying about it while making it worse by eating Tootsie Roll Pops and pistachio nuts in her bunk.

Her mother became very alarmed by Gilda's weight gain. Henrietta did not realize it had been partially her own odd lifestyle that made Gilda eat to cope. So as Gilda began at Liggett School, Henrietta forced Gilda onto her first of many, many diets. In the ignorance of those days, diets often included diet pills, "to deaden your appetite." On doctor's orders, Gilda began to take Dexedrine when she was only ten years old. It was not unusual in that pill-popping era for a patient to take as many as ten diet pills a day. In Gilda, it provoked major mood swings that later caused the doctors to tell her to quit taking them.

The end of her family's nomadism and the beginning of Liggett was a major turning point in Gilda's life. Liggett was located in a dark brick building in a vaguely English style that had been built in the twenties by Louis Kahn, the celebrated architect. There were about two hundred students from kindergarten through twelfth grade. Gilda loved the school. She made many friends, the first she had ever really had outside her family and Dibby.

She also loved her teacher, Miss Cole, whom she had for fifth and sixth grades. Miss Cole was "a charming Irish leprechaun," according to Ellen, who was one year behind Gilda. Miss Cole spoke with a thick brogue in which she told hair-raising stories of her life in Ireland through various rebellions where guns had been shot off right above her head.

Gilda wrote that she loved Miss Cole not only for her great stories but also because she rewarded academic achievement with chances for creativity. If you did well in math, you got to be in Miss Cole's oil-painting class. If you stood out in geography, you could study ballroom dancing. It was thanks to Miss Cole that Gilda always led when dancing.

Terese Davies Duell, a Liggett classmate, remembers Gilda as playful and studious:

"Thinking of Gilda is picturing a perennial smile and sparkling brown eyes laughing over an insightful quip she has just made. . . . A brow knitted in pensive thought as Miss Lothrop, our English teacher, helps us interpret Milton. . . . Or, as Miss Brown, our music teacher, leads us through a 'host of golden daffodils,' Gilda is mouthing her favorite catchphrase of the time:

" 'Are you kidding me, or what?' "

Gilda became an excellent student, and she always said that she found herself and formed her personality at Liggett School.

"Because I went to an all-girls' school," she once told an interviewer, "a lot of my energy was focused, instead of being successful and popular with guys, on being creative and witty and funny. You were better liked, not by who you were dating or if you were a cheerleader or what clothes you had, but if you were funny. It was just what was reinforced more. . . . I mean it was the whole thing, uniforms and field hockey."

Gilda was a strong, enthusiastic competitor in field hockey, throwing her arms above her head and shouting loudly when her team scored. She also enjoyed basketball, which she played well at Liggett, and student government—she was on the school's budget committee and was vice president of the senior class.

She stayed at Liggett from fifth grade until high school graduation, with the exception of her junior year, when she went to Mumford, then the predominantly Jewish public high school in Detroit. It later became famous on Eddie

Murphy's sweatshirt in *Beverly Hills Cop*, but in those days it was strictly cake eaters. Gilda went to Mumford that year because, in spite of all that creativity and wit, she wanted to meet boys.

"Liggett was a desert if you wanted to meet boys," Ellen said. "Especially if you had gone there since fifth grade, you didn't even know a single boy. You'd get a date to the senior prom mostly as a service."

But after one year at Mumford, Gilda decided to go back to Liggett for her senior year because she missed the traditions she had gotten so involved in.

She missed singing alto in a double quartet, and she especially missed her first efforts at serious acting on the school's dramatics board, Symmathetea, of which she was vice president. She had been active in drama right from the beginning, being in plays and working on crews. She was considered a ham and the class clown. When she was a senior, she directed a mystery called *Anti-clockwise*. It was a serious drama, but for some reason, under Gilda's direction, the audience began to giggle halfway through and continued laughing until the end. Even to a veteran director the unwanted sound of audience laughter is a horrifying experience. Gilda stayed out of school for two days in embarrassment.

At Liggett, Gilda played Tully Bascombe in *The Mouse That Roared*. She always got the male parts because even then she had a very strong, penetrating deep voice.

It was during her years at Liggett that, in addition to discovering her femininity, Gilda also first discovered she could make people laugh at will. She learned her lifelong axiom of comedy: all she had to do was say something *true* in a certain tone of voice and *fast* enough to take the listener by surprise. They would invariably laugh. It was like hitting their knees with that little rubber hammer—

it was a natural reflex, "Dibby's reflex," something involuntary.

At Liggett, Gilda's introspective side also had a chance to flourish. She once wrote an essay entitled "Countenance":

> Speak to me and I'll close my eyes. I want to hear your words and know not what lies in your face or physical appearance. Thus I will judge you by the thoughts you express and the ideas which you utter . . . if you should ever be revealed as someone of a different color, creed or race than myself, it will make no difference, for my eyes are closed to these and my ears and heart and mind will see rightly.

Her classmates remember Gilda for her intelligence, warmth, leadership, and humor. Terese Davies Duell says: "If Gilda was not the soul of wit, she was the heart of it."

The yearbook caption under her senior picture really expresses the essence of Gilda:

> The angel that presided o'er my birth
> Said, "Little creature formed of joy and mirth—
> Go, love without the help of anything on earth."

Gilda had a comic riff about her childhood, which she tried out for her friends with the idea that it might make the basis of a comedy sketch. It went something like this:

"When I was a little girl, I used to lie in bed and ask myself, 'All right, how about it, Gilda, are you glad you're a girl, or do you wish you were a boy?'

"I said, 'Boys have to go in the army, get in mud, wear heavy stuff, and kill people. That is not my idea of fun.'

"I love being a woman. You can cry. You get to wear pants now. You can always sit and think when you go to the bathroom. If you're on a boat and it's going to sink, you get to go on the rescue boat first. You get to wear cute clothes. Being a woman must be a great thing, or so many men wouldn't be wanting to do it now.

"One great thing about not being superior, you get to change yourself. Wear high-heeled shoes, make yourself taller, put makeup on.

"And you get to give up."

Although she would have been horrified to be thought of as a feminist, or any kind of *-ist*, Gilda from her Liggett days on was quite certain that a woman could do anything. She always needed her man for love, but never for "success in the world."

As a preteen Gilda had her fair share of curiosity about sex. In that era Detroit Jewish girls rarely had sexual experience by high school and even more rarely had "gone all the way."

Sex was, naturally, the prime topic of conversation at many Liggett slumber parties. One of these parties lasted five days. It was held in a cabin in Indian River, in Michigan's wild and woolly Upper Peninsula. There were four girls, Gilda, Ellen, Ellen's sister Patty, and Kay Mark, whose parents owned the cabin.

The girls had remembered to bring toothbrushes and clothing but had neglected to bring any music. All they had to listen to were the same ten 45s that they happened to find in the house. They committed all of them to memory. From that moment on, whenever they heard "Sea of Love" or "Will You Still Love Me Tomorrow," they would suddenly be transported back to that week in Michigan, when they had promised one another they would never, ever, ever kiss a boy unless they had already decided to marry him.

That was Gilda at age twelve.

By age fourteen, Gilda was giving Ellen Frank advice on kissing.

"If you're outta town, then make the most of it," she advised. "That's how you get experience and can still keep your reputation."

Ellen recalled this one night on a date, as she was parked outside the Detroit city limits in a two-seater Corvair with a guy who went to another school.

"The guy yanked me over and stuck his mouth on mine," Ellen recalled with a grimace. "It was yucky. But I kept thinking of what Gilda had said: 'If you're outta town, make the most of it.' So I kept on. In fact, I had even heard of this French kissing, so I stuck my tongue in the guy's mouth. He was so shocked he didn't do anything. And I kept repeating Gilda's words to myself."

At this age Gilda and Ellen spent a lot of time going to Detroit's great arena, Cobo Hall, to listen to music. All the great Motown bands played there. Once Gilda and Ellen got lost in Cobo Hall looking for the bathroom. They were wandering through the corridors when a guy in a loud gold shirt approached them.

"Hey, girls. I'm Del Shannon!" he said importantly.

"I don't care who you are!" Gilda snapped, and Del Shannon backed off.

The summer before high school, Gilda and Ellen flew to New York to visit Ellen's father. They both smoked.

"Gilda said to me, 'If we're going to smoke, don't let's both smoke at the same time. It'll look more mature if only one person smokes at a time,' " Ellen said.

"Gilda used to go cross-eyed when she smoked, because she was trying to see the cigarette and see how cool she looked smoking!"

Years later, when America as a whole was becoming

disgusted with smoking, Gilda persisted. She loved to smoke, and she said, with an undercurrent of mock anger that made it funny:

"At least I have a say in my death. At least I'm causing it, instead of having it sneak up on me!"

When she said things like that, she had in mind to use her neurotic way of life as a source for her comedy material. In those days her whole mission was to milk her life for humor.

On "Saturday Night," for instance, she did sketches about breast cancer, carrying a big clutch bag over her chest, just two years after her mother had fought off the disease.

Gilda had been hooked on saccharin for twenty years. When it was banned, suspected of being carcinogenic, Gilda sang a love song to her sweetener that became a comedy classic, "Goodbye Saccharin":

> I can look everywhere from Arkansas to Akron;
> But, sugar, there's no sugar substitute to substitute for saccharin. . . .

"She never got in trouble," Ellen recalled. "But no one ever thought of her as a goody two-shoes either. She never sucked up to people. It all came from this extraordinary sense of kindness she had."

At fourteen, a little thinner than before and a lot funnier, Gilda and Ellen went to a live performance of "Lunch with Soupy Sales," a slapstick comedy program that was then breaking all records on local Detroit television. "Telegram for Mr. Sales!" became one of the stock phrases of Detroit youth in the fifties and early sixties. On Soupy's show it was always the signal that the star was about to get hit in the face with a cream pie.

On the day Gilda went, Soupy had promised "A Busload of Stars," and sure enough Edd "Kookie" Byrnes, Troy Donahue, and Connie Stevens were Soupy's guests. The young, star-struck Gilda walked away with their autographs.

She carried Troy Donahue's autograph in her wallet for the next sixteen years and would show it on demand. She stopped carrying it only when she finally realized she had become more famous than he was.

By age seventeen, out of a combination of social necessity and hormones, most grudgingly, she had, in lieu of actually "doing it," developed a tentative interest in alternative styles of taking care of business. The interest had been sparked by one guy, who had gone out with a number of the Mumford and Liggett girls, including the stunning Patty Frank, Ellen's older sister.

After Patty, this nameless but important fellow dated Gilda for quite a while during her senior year. He never stopped trying to get lucky. Gilda was horrified yet fascinated by the idea of sex, especially of the kinky kind being suggested by the guy. She steadfastly refused.

But the man had a plan. He knew how desperately Gilda wanted to be invited to the Liggett senior prom. The year before, he had taken Patty Frank, and it had been the social success of 1963.

So he invited Gilda to her Liggett senior prom. She was thrilled.

"We recycled, even then," quips Ellen.

In the ensuing days, threatening to revoke his invitation, the man extracted a promise from Gilda. After great finagling, he managed to convince Gilda to agree to give him "first tongue" on the night of the prom.

She had demurred with great insistence, but he had

finally blackmailed her into promising to give head *on* date certain, in exchange *for* date certain. For her part, she had extracted a solemn promise from him to make sure that on that appointed night his tool would be surgically sterile, even cleaner than her mother's kitchen floor. To accomplish this, she had not economized on her already large repertoire of facial postures to drive home the point of just how unsanitary she found the entire process.

Mr. Nameless, though undoubtedly a cad for extracting such a slobbery promise, proved to be more of a gentleman than some of Gilda's subsequent lovers.

After the stiff-necked dance, when the time finally came in the backseat of Nameless's '58 Chevy, Gilda, all faces and nervous jokes, finally unzipped and prepared to lip. Shutting her eyes as he carefully pulled out his pubescent peter, she was more or less mentally prepared for slavering and slobbering.

But wait a minute! What's that smell? Her eyes flew open. Mint? Menthol? Stannous fluoride?

The saliva in her mouth turned to laughter when she observed that Nameless, ever thoughtful, had painstakingly covered every cubic inch of his tumescent teenage dong with sticky, smelly white stuff—toothpaste!

Paging Roseanne Roseannadanna. . . .

Those were indeed the early days of the sexual revolution. By the time Gilda began college, birth control pills, Lippes loops, and the like had changed the world.

Gilda soon threw caution to the winds. As she has written herself, at age nineteen she got pregnant and had to have an illegal abortion.

The way she told it to us, her friends, it sounded like the classic lament of the Jewish princess:

"I have to have a little minor surgery."

She would vaguely gesture toward her belly, and I was so naive I thought it had something to do with diet pills, which I knew she had taken, on and off, since she was ten years old. There was also some mention of that curious woman's problem that seemed to be sweeping Ann Arbor, "cystitis." Only Ellen and Kitty knew the truth.

All life experiences, good or bad, leave their marks on one's body. Every bit of suffering and strain goes right into the bone marrow. Unless it's gently unkinked, worked out, let go of, it stays there forever. Gilda was never quite the same from then on. Her basic color changed. Younger she had been even more rosy, radiant, and beautiful. After the abortion, although still lively, perky, charming, and lovely, another very slight touch of wistful sadness crept into her demeanor. That tinge of sadness was one of the things that made her humor so appealing. Often she told sad stories and everybody laughed.

She has said that that abortion was probably the root cause of her 1985 miscarriage, after she was married to Gene. Although she felt there might be a relation, medical specialists familiar with her case disagree, saying it probably did not malign her ultimately unhealthy reproductive organs. In any case, who it was that made her pregnant none of us were ever able to confirm.

Building directly on her interests at Liggett, in Ann Arbor Gilda really began to hone her talent as an actress and comedian. Even though Roseanne Roseannadanna once appeared on the cover of the alumni bulletin, Gilda never exactly graduated from the University of Michigan. But she spent six years there studying drama, as well as clowning around in person, on the radio, and in the theater.

While others were manning and womanning the picket lines, Gilda was being brilliant as the fairy princess in a play put on for the children of Ann Arbor at the Lydia Mendelsohn Theater. All who saw her perform will never forget the way she seemed to evanesce and go partially invisible as she waved her wand.

Dave Berson, an old mutual friend, remembers it this way:

"I didn't really know anything about Gilda's aspirations until I attended a play in which she appeared. . . . I had no idea what to expect, but from the time she appeared onstage, Gilda became a very different person for me. She didn't say anything beforehand, but she had the lead, playing a beautiful fairy princess. And from the opening moment of her performance she captivated everyone in the theater, young and old alike. I can still remember Gilda onstage in a blue chiffon gown and the kids in the audience on the edge of their seats. Gilda lit up the whole theater. From that day, I knew she had something special and that she was very serious about her acting craft. . . .

"The Gilda I saw at that little children's play could have very well been a fine dramatic actress, someone who had wonderful contributions to make in many areas of drama. People will remember her for all her crazy characters, but there was a lot more there. I treasure the memory of that little children's play and feel privileged I got a chance to see that side of Gilda."

Her whimsical fairy princess costume made an indelible impression on Gilda, as well as on audience members like Dave Berson and me. In New York many years later, in a photo session at the Ronald Feldman Fine Arts Gallery, after spending the morning looking at Buckminster Fuller's *Goldilocks* exhibit, Gilda donned nearly the identical costume for her first appearance as a magazine "cover girl." She graced a special issue of *Rags* wearing a multicolored chiffon skirt and pink ballet slippers and carrying a magic wand with a star on top. She's wearing a gold "fairy princess" crown and is accompanied by a goose sitting on top of a golden L'eggs egg.

The caption read, "The Goose That Glows." In a blurb alongside, Gilda mentioned her "whimsical fairy princess skirt," adding that it came right out of Fiorucci's window and that the shoes had come from Capezio.

Gilda was thrilled by her first appearance as a cover girl. She worked very hard on her photo sessions, and she also wrote an introductory blurb entitled: "47 Secret Thoughts of a Model!!!":

> *Rags* asked me to be on their cover because they had thought about gold being all the rage this year in fashion, and their minds went gold . . . gilded . . . Gilda!!! So they called me. I said yes because I'd seen the cover on their special preview issue of Lauren Hutton with a fly on her nose. I figured I'd look exactly like her, without the fly. I was going to be a model.
>
> FEBRUARY 9, 8 PM: I started the purification of my body. I took a two-hour bath, did my toenails, did my nails, put on my prettiest nightgown, took a Valium and went to bed.
>
> FEBRUARY 10, 7 AM: I woke up and I was still clean, but a little groggy. I took a cab to Xavier, New York on 57th Street. I waited outside on the stairs because I was afraid to go in 'til I saw somebody I knew. Believe me, Edward, my hairdresser, was charming. But I have a desperate fear of flying into a mirror in beauty parlors. After a minor temper tantrum, I allowed him to trim my hair, wash it, and kink it with a curling iron while Sandra put dots on my nose, outlined

> my lips and made my eyes look not so close together. They made Gilda into Marisa Berenson. And it only took three, four hours. Then I spent the whole day as a model with Arnold following me around with a brush in his hand, and people pinning, primping and hovering over me. I couldn't believe it. . . . I forgot to eat!

This was one of Gilda's favorite photo sessions. It lasted three days. Part of it took place on the roof of Gilda's building on Charles Street. According to the photographer, Carolyn Schultz:

"It is very hard to light the roof of a New York apartment building. The black tar absorbs all the light. So I had laid down yards of silver Mylar to bounce the light back."

To apprise the superintendent of why there was so much commotion on top of the building, Carolyn wrote a note that said:

"We are shooting Gilda on the roof!"

The super thought it was a terrorist message and was in the act of dialing the Sixth Precinct when Gilda walked in dressed all in gold. She and the super both laughed. Gilda went up to the roof and lay down lengthwise on the silver Mylar in a kind of sultry pose.

"It shot sparks all over the Village," Carolyn said. "Gilda reminded me of Shirley Eaton in *Goldfinger*."

The rooftop photo of Gilda in the gold suit illustrated the very best article ever done on her, an interview with Rosie Shuster, a fellow member of the "SNL" cast and writing staff. Here's a sample, preserved for posterity:

> ROSIE: Gilda, how do you select your wardrobe?
> GILDA: I don't have a wardrobe. I have a history. Things that went through stuff with me.

ROSIE: Do you hate any of your clothes?

GILDA: I hate clothes that let me down. You know, the ones that are never the same after the first washing. I love blouses with puffy sleeves but they always come back from the cleaners flat and wilted and smelling of how much they cost. Also I hate materials that retain perspiration that you know you didn't make yourself. The ones you always have to smell before you wear or pour a lot of perfume on it. And my Mom always said that someone who smelled of perfume was hiding something.

ROSIE: Has being on television changed your life?

GILDA: No, it's changed my hair. . . .

ROSIE: Do you have an exercise regimen you'd like to share with the readers?

GILDA: In the morning I do a hundred jumping jacks, then I do a hundred skip ropes but I stopped using the rope 'cause it took too long if I missed. I just pretend I have the rope. Then I make the bed, picking up the pillows off the floor without bending my knees. There are four pillows. Then I do 30 leg kicks and 30 bump and grinds backwards and forwards and then I take a bath and think aloud whether I should add another exercise to my regimen.

ROSIE: What is your favorite accessory?

GILDA: My contact lenses. Because if I didn't wear them I'd have to wear big, thick glasses.

ROSIE: Anything else?

GILDA: My clip-on mittens.

During the production of this splendid Gilda cover, she

welcomed the photo crew into her apartment for a drink after the shoot on the roof. She spent the whole time speaking just to Carolyn and her assistant. But as the crowd was about to leave, Gilda said good-bye to each one of them personally, shaking their hands and kissing them and remembering accurately the names of each person—a total of at least fifteen. They were astounded at her memory and her grace.

"I'm a cover girl!" she crowed as she showed the magazine to me when it came out.

Gilda was so proud that she posted the fairy princess/goose picture on the "Saturday Night" bulletin board, adding, in her distinctive rounded handwriting with little arrowheads:

"Lorne, I'm happy. Love, Gilda."

She later used the photograph to make postcards.

The goose was a very Gilda touch that derived from her lifelong fantasy of living on a farm. Often, in Ann Arbor, we would talk about what animals we would have.

"I'd have ducks and geese and sheep and goats and cows and horses and dogs and cats and lots and lots of children," Gilda would say with a rapturous smile on her face, her eyes sparkling.

Even though she grew up in a quasi-theatrical family and in the atmosphere of show business, Gilda never foresaw that she would become a big star. She always imagined herself ending up something like Dibby: wearing a print dress with mobs of kids and animals, rocking on the front porch with her fantasy husband, watching life and the neighbors go by. It was right out of Norman Rockwell. Even after she achieved stardom, she was ready to give it all up for a housewifely life as Mrs. Gene Wilder.

All her life Gilda's enormous reservoirs of love and money went out to her friends.

"You can always come to me for money," she said to me, and I was proud that I never did. It wasn't that I didn't need it. But I did not want to take advantage of her generosity. Her friendship was ample reward.

Long before she became internationally famous, however, many people knew she was wealthy, having inherited the Radner fortune. They did not hesitate to hit her up for funds. She would never make loans, but she never refused to give money to anyone, as far as I have been able to find out.

She especially treasured old school and camp friends.

Once in Ann Arbor she and I and a bunch of friends—who have remained friends to this day—went on a picnic in a stand of woods behind the university campus called "Dell-High Park."

There were three cars, and as we departed after the picnic, somehow Gilda got left behind. Each thought she was in another car.

When we got back to Haven Street, the telephone was ringing. It was Gilda, in tears. She had been sitting forlornly on the side of the road, crying her eyes out, until someone had given her a ride to a telephone.

Of course, we drove back to pick her up. She was still in tears.

She roundly cursed all her "friends" for forgetting about her. Over the next twenty years she would never hesitate to mention the incident whenever that crowd got uppity. But she gave nearly all of them money without any questions.

5

Gilda and *Godspell*

"And the laughter, that's my unemployment insurance"

GILDA FREQUENTLY MADE SPECIAL EFFORTS TO ENSURE THE happiness and material well-being of her friends, even after she became world-famous. But there was one episode that left her feeling deeply ashamed:

Not long after our experiences in Paris, Gilda ran away with Jeffrey Rubinoff, her best friend's sister's husband.

Jeffrey had married the stunning Patty Frank, who had graduated from Liggett and "Mr. Nameless" to become Jeff's college sweetheart.

"Jeff and Patty had eloped and at first had one of those 'huggy-duggy' relationships where you couldn't get one off the other's lap" as Ellen describes it.

They had plans for the future: to finish school at the University of Oklahoma, where Jeffrey was getting his MFA, and then to "make the scene" in Toronto, Jeffrey's hometown, have babies, etc.—"the whole catastrophe," as Zorba the Greek once put it.

For reasons best known to herself, it was just then, in the early years of their marriage, that Patty chose to step out.

Jeffrey was devastated, "went nuts," and came to Ellen for "marriage counseling." At the time, Ellen was living upstairs from Gilda on Monroe Street in Ann Arbor. Ellen and Jeffrey had always been close friends and confidants, but now Ellen felt strangely divided giving marital advice. She sympathized with Jeffrey but did not like taking a position against her own sister.

"So I clammed up," she said.

Desperate, in a way only sensitive artists can get, Jeffrey began to seek counseling elsewhere—in this case downstairs, in Gilda's apartment. They, too, had become close friends.

In the subsequent week, a week when teenage Vietnam War veterans were returning to campus wounded and bandaged, and Michigan State Police were firing pepper gas at student protesters, Gilda and Jeff closed the windows, shut out the world, and became closer still.

Gilda's farm fantasy resurfaced, and she suddenly longed for a simple existence as a housewife and mother of Jeffrey's children.

After eight days of this intensive soul burning, in a smashing dramatic entrance, Patty suddenly arrived on the scene, demanding to know who was sleeping with her husband.

Just as suddenly, in a major piece of upstaging, Gilda and Jeff announced *they* were toddling off together to Toronto, where Jeff intended to file for divorce!

Even though she had precipitated the situation, Patty was crushed. According to Ellen, she soon suffered a sort of nervous breakdown. Curiously, she stayed in touch, and still stays in touch, with Jeffrey's sister, although not at all with him.

Ellen was also devastated. She had been Gilda's closest friend since the fifth grade. After this she did not speak to Gilda for five years.

For a while, in spite of the awkward and steamy situation, Gilda and Jeffrey seemed like a brilliant match. Jeffrey was and still is a very talented artist and sculptor, not to mention rich, handsome, and extremely bright. Unfortunately for them, he has a rather dictatorial, though lovable, personality. After a few months Gilda began calling me, very depressed. She began to complain that she was constantly fighting with her new lover. The marriage part was not happening. She was learning to cook and helping him with his art shows, going to night school at the University of Toronto, and taking correspondence courses from the University of Wisconsin Extension to try to finish her degree, and also taking arts and crafts classes.

Once during this period I telephoned her and asked what they were doing. She answered with something that I knew was right out of Jeffrey Rubinoff's mouth, not hers:

"Making art."

She was living out the fantasy of the Ann Arbor hippie-wife and hating it. From her point of view the only positive benefit of this period was that Jeff had insisted she get slim, and she began to do so.

Not long after they eloped, she telephoned, sounding frantic, and told me:

"I'm going crazy! Jeffrey is *refusing to let me be funny*!"

She sounded stunned. I was stunned too, because I thought she was the funniest person in the world.

"I can't stand it! He actually does not like my jokes!" she sputtered. "Can you fuckin' believe it?"

Worried about her, I accepted an invitation they extended and went to Toronto. The first night, they took me to dinner at the best restaurant in town, Three Small Rooms.

"This is our life," Gilda said. "We eat here three times a week." She did not sound happy, except with the quality of the food, which was far above what we had eaten in Paris a year or so before.

At dinner Jeffrey scared the living *bosta* out of me with one of his patented black leather diatribes on nuclear war, the extinction of the human race, and the necessity of making art to fight all this. He was heavy, he still is heavy, and he's my brother. But Gilda was my sister, and she was totally bummed out.

"I went on this horrible progression," she remembered of this era, "from thinking I was going to die to thinking there was going to be a nuclear war, and then I settled on a fear of airplanes that lasted for six years."

Jeffrey can do that to a person, even a smart one. Especially a smart one.

Their typical knot went like this: Gilda would make a crack, and Jeff would say, in a sort of mock gruff tone, "You don't have to put on a show for me." She was crushed.

Jeffrey once said about the same epoch:

"When you marry for a second time, you usually become the man your first wife wanted."

Their life was not exactly your model of upper-class Jewish domesticity. True, they were living in the obligatory white condo tower with a gracefully curving front facade. Their apartment was done in leather modern. But instead of tchotchkes, the apartment was full of huge steel sculptures and stacks of *National Lampoon*s. Those belonged to Jeffrey.

It was policed regularly by a tiny Yorkshire terrier named Snuffy, "the Insufferable." She was Gilda's.

Gilda and Jeffrey made a brave stab at couplehood. But it always ended in failure and conflict and oft unappreciated, if not unintentional, humor.

Once while I was there visiting, Jeffrey bought three pounds of meat for Gilda to cook one night for our dinner. Even though she was gamely playing "peasant domestic," she hated to cook and at that time did not really know more than broiling meat. But she broiled the meat, and it smelled so good that she began to eat it. She ate and ate and gave a bit to Snuffy, and before she knew what had happened, all the meat was gone.

Jeffrey returned from his studio later in the day. The smell of the meat was still in the air, and when he learned it had vanished, Jeff began to berate Gilda.

Gilda in turn scolded Snuffy.

"Snuffy must have eaten it," Gilda said to Jeffrey. "All three pounds of it. You bad dog," she said, in a mock severe tone.

Snuffy, the perfect straight dog, tried to tuck her tiny tail between her legs.

Jeffrey looked at Gilda skeptically, then at the cowering Snuffy. He picked Snuffy up with one hand, which the dog promptly tried to bite. Jeff gritted his teeth and tossed the terrier onto the bathroom scale.

The tiny dog weighed just a fraction over three pounds.

"If this is the dog," Jeffrey shouted, "where is the meat?"

And Gilda answered in an equally loud voice an octave higher:

"And if this is the meat, where is the dog?"

Gilda loved Snuffy dearly, and when the frisky little dog died she bought another Yorkshire terrier just like her. This one she named Sparkle; she has written about her at length in *It's Always Something.*

Whether Jeff confessed to liking her jokes or not, he was a charter subscriber to and great fan of *National Lampoon*, a magazine Gilda soon contributed to in spirit and later in writing. Eventually, in New York, she became a mainstay of "The National Lampoon Radio Hour," a precursor of "Saturday Night."

But Jeffrey, in spite of an ego the size of the tallest

building in Toronto, was, after all, a Canadian and spelled *humor* with two *us*. Jeffrey had already realized that he wanted a traditional wife, not a transcendental wit. Being pretty funny himself (he once said, "Everything I know I learned from a talking duck!") and cutting quite a dash as an aspiring artist/sculptor, perhaps he did not relish competition from such a talented comic genius. Nevertheless, Jeff would be the first to appreciate the irony that, while Gilda was hooking rugs in his living room in 1969 and hating it, she was watching something called "The Hart and Lorne Terrific Hour" on Canadian television. It was a comedy show, not all that funny, but it starred this interesting guy who Gilda said looked like a deflated David Crosby. His name was Lorne Michaels.

One summer, at the climax of this daymare, we went for a picnic on a beautiful island in the Toronto River. Gilda was glum, very depressed, one of the only times I had ever seen her like this.

She was now openly defiant toward Jeffrey and did not hesitate to put him down in front of me. He is a very proud guy, and finally he snapped back.

"Look, Gilda. It's up to you. Decide what you want. Decide who you want."

I felt quite uncomfortable observing this domestic battle, so I feebly tried to make a joke of it.

"Yeah, Gilda," I said. "Decide. For instance, if Jeffrey and I were both drowning in this river, who would you save?"

Gilda thought for a moment, then broke out into a big smile. She turned to Jeff and said, in a voice like a velvet shiv:

"Tell me, Jeffrey. Do you know how to swim?"

After sixteen months or so of this mercurial relationship,

Gilda and Jeff split up. Gilda and Snuffy, alone, decided to stay in Canada and look for new worlds to conquer.

Gilda blew off steam from her Jeffrey fiasco in a highly original way. She became addicted to bingo. For months she went practically every night to a different church bingo parlor.

It was not unusual for her to play sixteen bingo cards at once.

The more cards, the better your chances are, she thought.

Gilda's bingo binge has always struck me as very curious. She played like a demon in Canada and then seemed to slow down for a while. But even years later, when she was very famous, she would occasionally feel the compulsion to play, and disguised in an assortment of wigs, hats, and glasses, she would sneak off to a bingo game at some church in Long Island or New Jersey.

In Canada the early-bird games began at six-thirty in the evening. Gilda often played five nights a week, usually staying until eleven o'clock. She brought her own plastic chips, which she carried in a pink and blue bag she had crocheted herself.

"I think she liked bingo because it gave her a chance to be with old people," remembered Kitty Shannon, who moved in with Gilda in Toronto right around this time.

At the bingo parlor, along with all the other players, Gilda smoked one cigarette after another. She gorged on potato chips and hot dogs.

"Once I was so intent on my sixteen cards that instead of reaching into my bag of counters I put my hand in the mustard," she recalled with a chuckle.

The most Gilda ever won at bingo was $250. She undoubtedly paid out a lot more than that in entry fees and taxi fares. But she loved to go, I believe, because it gave her a chance to exercise her powers of observation, it allowed her to be with people who reminded her of Dibby, and it gave her license to smoke and eat as much as she could cram into her mouth.

After Gilda left Jeffrey, she tried hard to befriend Patty and Ellen again. Five years later, when Ellen resumed speaking to her, Gilda claimed that her own guilt at being the home wrecker had played a part in her decision to leave Jeff.

What happened to Jeffrey Rubinoff: in *another* week-long whirlwind courtship, he ran off with a dark-haired beauty named Darlene Haber, whom he met, curiously enough, at my house—Frazzle Top Farm, in the Adirondack Mountains. They married and moved to Hornby Island, British Columbia, to have children, raise buffalo, and, of course, make art. Their daughter, Lila, was born in 1976. After ten years of marriage they divorced. Jeffrey is now living with a new girlfriend, still on Hornby. He's still making steel art and looking for a mountainside on which to place his futuristic sculptures, where they may last into an era that will finally appreciate them.

In 1970 Gilda moved out of the white condo to 77 Pears Street, a two-story Victorian town house with a fenced-in garden and backyard. Gilda used to love sitting on the back steps, facing the garden and sunbathing, although out of fear of skin cancer she made very sure to take only the early morning sun and never to get burned. One of her favorite features was the huge master bathroom, as large as the bedroom. Gilda filled the house with old burnished knotty pine furniture, numerous calico prints, Early American quilts, and brightly colored afghans she crocheted herself. The place also had a lot of mirrors.

She needed the mirrors to practice her body work, since for the next year or two she put herself on Weight Watchers and also regularly performed as a mime and clown for children, earning sixty dollars a week and thoroughly enjoying every moment of it.

"She needed Weight Watchers," Kitty recalled. "Her weight went down from 145 to 128. She never really got fat again. She looked great and got gorgeous legs from her diet. Before that, she had had no legs at all."

Gilda has seconded this by saying that before this time she never wore jeans because she actually had legs but not ones that could get into any pants. Starting in Toronto, she began to wear pants tucked into boots, far in advance of fashion, and there she finally got rid of her hated thigh chafe guards, an accessory her mother had insisted on.

Because of the millstone of her weight problems, for the first time in her life, and practically the last, in Toronto Gilda decided she really needed to learn how to cook, something more than just broiling meat. Kitty was already an excellent cook, and she taught Gilda how to make her first real dish: lemon chicken.

"You take a whole chicken," Kitty told her, demonstrating. "Wash and dry it. Squeeze lemon juice all over it. Cut up some lemons. Then you mince some garlic and onions. You stuff the chicken with lemon peel and garlic and onions and rub it all over with olive oil. You add thyme, salt, and pepper and roast it for an hour."

It was, Kitty recalled, Gilda's favorite dish for years—except, of course, for tuna fish.

Gilda and Kitty loved shopping for food together in Toronto's fanciest food markets.

"She would always pick the nicest-looking vegetables and fruits," Kitty remembered. "She didn't want to eat anything that didn't look absolutely beautiful and perfect. We'd sometimes drive for miles to find the perfect avocado or tomato or something. And she'd always buy the most expensive one. She didn't have any notion of saving money when it came to food."

Kitty also recalls that because of her food-cleanup habits Gilda impressed her as "political" in these years:

"In her own unique way, of course. For instance, she would always sort the garbage in Toronto. She was into recycling before anyone had even invented the word. She was also very into 'women's liberation,' but not with rhetoric. I'm sure she never used the phrase *women's liberation.* She just felt that a woman could do as well as a man, or better. She was real low-key about it, and her politics always had a human slant. She would never read, you know, *Ramparts* or anything. Her favorite magazine was *Cosmo.* But she was as political as anyone else."

A few months after the break with Jeffrey, Gilda and Kitty had gone to a small avant-garde theater on Yonge Street in Toronto to see a new musical. When Gilda entered the theater, she said to herself: "Eureka!" She knew where she wanted to be. Of course it did not hurt that on the way in Gilda had fallen in love with the ticket taker.

She confided as much to Kitty when they went home. Kitty, you should know, is a stunning blond with an incisive intelligence. She has the fire of her Italian mother and the gift of blarney of her Irish father, with a heart as big and clear and warm as Lake Superior during Indian summer. She was always one hundred percent loyal to Gilda, and she immediately resolved to help Gilda get her man.

The very next day, Kitty returned to the theater. The ticket taker, whose name she soon learned was Marcus, was still there.

"So I picked him up," Kitty admitted without a blush, "and took him home for Gilda. They got along great, spending day and night doing bits together. He was a good comic. He drank six Cokes a day. We laughed till we peed."

In less time than it takes to say "Samuel P. Marchbanks," Gilda got a job in the same theater doing pantomime stories for elementary school children.

Gilda had found happiness at last. She was in love, she was in the theater, and she was driving a troupe of four clowns from school to school in her own car, a blue Volvo with a gray interior.

On one of my last visits to Toronto, Gilda asked me to help her work a gag on some of the parents who came to pick up their children. Both parents and children loved it.

First, Gilda had me act as shill. I went up to a couple of prosperous-looking parents and told them if they wanted to see something funny they should just check out what happened when they offered Gilda the choice between a big tip and a small tip.

The parents were intrigued, and they went up to Gilda with a coin in each hand—a quarter in one, a dime in the other.

"Gilda," they said, "which coin would you like for a tip?"

Gilda unhesitatingly took the dime, and the parents cracked up with laughter.

A second set of parents was looking on, and they wanted to try the same thing. Again Gilda took the smaller coin.

The parents again snickered up their sleeves, and the kids began to laugh at seeing their parents laugh.

Before long, nearly all the parents at the school were offering Gilda coins or even bills. Again, if offered the choice between a ten-dollar bill and a one-dollar bill, Gilda took the single.

I couldn't believe what I was seeing. I watched for a while and finally could stand it no longer.

"Gilda!" I expostulated. "I don't care if it *is* Canadian

money! For God's sake take the *bigger* coin or the *bigger* bill! You'll make more money. And you won't have them laughing *at* you, just *with* you."

"No, Dave," Gilda replied. "Then I wouldn't make any money at all. They only offer me the money to show how stupid I am!

"And the laughter, that's my unemployment insurance. That means I can keep working here next week!"

By now she was twenty-three years old and had just discovered you could have a job being funny. Being the poor little rich girl who had recently "busted a trust," she did not need a job at all, but her tribulations with Jeffrey had convinced her she had no future as a domestic and should get out there and work.

She saw *Hair* that year and also went to a Monty Python concert in Toronto that changed her life. Gilda suddenly understood there could be a whole new direction for clowning and performance comedy, something along the lines of what *National Lampoon* was doing in print. After the concert she waited backstage for Michael Palin to come out.

When he did, "my heart fluttered, I stumbled over my words, and then I really made a fool out of myself—I asked him to marry me.

"He looked at me idiotically, like I had just handed him a warm turd. So I said,

" 'What's the matter? Haven't you ever seen a fool before?' "

During this period in Toronto, Gilda began doing charity work, continuing her family tradition of philanthropy. She worked with blind people, reading them funny stories. She tried amateur physical therapy with the handicapped and spastics. Because of her constant battles with her own physical appearance, she always showed great tolerance for other people's weaknesses.

Kitty recalls: "I used to be very impatient with stupid people in those days. It used to drive me crazy. But Gilda always used to tell me: 'It's not their fault if they're stupid. Maybe they were just born with less brains than you. It's not their fault; you shouldn't blame them. You have to be more respectful with people.' "

Even after she became ill, Gilda retained this spirit. Kitty reports: "I visited her in Connecticut once when she was sick, and *she* ended up cheering *me*. She told me, 'You've got to be more positive. Give yourself credit for what you do well. Look for the blue sky.' "

It was vintage Gilda.

In 1972, Gilda saw a notice that open casting was about to begin for a Toronto company of *Godspell*. She worked hard on her audition by mastering her favorite song, "Zip-a-Dee-Doo-Dah."

She was chosen to be a member of a remarkable company of talented people: Paul Shaffer, Martin Short, Victor Garber, Eugene Levy, and Andrea Martin, all of whom went on to bigger and better things.

Gilda was especially delighted that she was admitted to Actors' Equity, the performer's union. She was indisputably now in show business, and she suddenly began to blossom.

She was intrigued by *Godspell* not only because it was her first professional job. Although she always considered herself unquestionably Jewish, she had also developed a strong feeling for Christian imagery. She had been brought up Jewish by her parents. She had gone to Sunday school and Hebrew school and learned to speak Hebrew after a fashion. But she also grew up in a predominantly Catholic neighborhood of Detroit. She very much enjoyed singing Easter and Christmas hymns in the choral groups at Liggett School. And Gilda frequently used to accompany Dibby to the Episcopalian church on Sundays. She was always intrigued by the concept that Jesus suffered for our sins. As she put it, "He took the rap for everyone."

At this time in Toronto, Gilda was supremely happy. She was free and twenty-five. Snuffy was free and four. She would hum "Day by Day" for hours and days on end, after "watching Him die for our sins eight times a week."

In the last three years of her life Gilda was forced to draw on the considerable spiritual strength she had stored up in these early days. When her illness did not surrender to inner or outer ministrations, she seriously and justly began to feel that she herself was pegged for a Jesus role. She used to muse that Jesus was Jewish and so was she.

"Why do I have to be Jesus? Why all this suffering in my life?" Gilda wailed from the heart in her book.

"Why am I marked for some kind of suffering that I see others aren't going through?" she continued.

"To make the connection to Jesus was not so farfetched because he certainly, as I hear tell, didn't deserve to die in such a gruesome way. . . . Once I even joked to people that I would give them a picture of me to hang over their bed, that I suffered for their sins and for whatever they did."

Some will say it is heretical to suggest that Gilda died for our sins. But she did. She did not die for her own. If anyone ever lived a close to sinless life, it was she. She did not deserve her cruel, painful fate. She was pure of heart, like the saints of old. She lived an exemplary life, resisting half a cornucopia of temptations. She regularly performed miracles. She died of her torments. She paid for her existence in blood.

After *Godspell*, Gilda joined the Toronto company of

Second City, that seminal comedy revue based in Chicago that has provided America with the bulk of its last thirty years of comic talent. There she worked with excellent performers like Dan Aykroyd, Eugene Levy, and Valri Bromfield. All the material was improvised. The only props they had to work with were a few chairs, a few hats, some clothing, and several pairs of glasses, to suggest character—the precursor of Gilda's future disguises.

Gilda was very nervous at these performances. The audience would throw out topics, and the performers had to think and write on their feet, using their tongues as pencils. She had to drink a beer and eat a bag of potato chips before she could go on. But when she went on, her clowning flowed forth—she was funny! She was a comedian!

The audiences loved her. They used to delight in throwing her weird topics, to see what off-the-wall stuff she could come up with.

"The toilet seat!" someone might shout from the floor.

Gilda would give one of her patented looks of bedazzlement, as if she were stumped beyond repair. Then, without missing a beat, she would walk offstage and come back on wearing an ankle-length skirt. As she walked on, she would pick up the hem of the skirt and shake it as if it were all wet, and the audience would shake with laughter.

Behind the scenes at Second City it was total bedlam.

"Gilda, be in this with me."

"Gilda, don't be in this with me."

"Gilda, will you work with me on this? Let's do this."

Gilda became a crucial part of the Second City crowd. That revue was about to reap a bumper crop of major talent. It was the crucible for Gilda's comedy. Here, among some of the finest comic minds of our generation, Gilda perfected her clowning art. It was through Second City that Gilda met John Belushi, Bill Murray, and Harold Ramis.

She eventually became quite a star in Canada, appearing in a number of CBC television productions for children. She got her first role in a movie, a one-line part as one of the chanting Nichiren Shoshu Buddhists in the Greenwich Village scene in *The Last Detail*, starring Jack Nicholson. It was also there in Canada that an ambitious Canadian producer/performer, a big fan of Second City named Lorne Michaels, first saw Gilda perform.

6

Jewish Girl from Detroit Storms New York

"And there's a girl *in the show"*

IN 1974, AFTER SIX YEARS NORTH OF THE BORDER, GILDA CAME to New York at the invitation of her Second City friend, playmate, and mentor John Belushi. The enfant terrible of Chicago, Belushi was readying an assault on the Big Apple. He had visited the Toronto company several times, first to make friends with and steal away Dan Aykroyd and then to nab Gilda to work on "The National Lampoon Radio Hour" and *The National Lampoon Show.*

Gilda called Belushi "the master of kamikaze comedy." He was not only a stand-up guy and a great talent; he was a good business strategist, and most important, he had a vision. It was he who, in 1974, decided to put together a resident company to do "The National Lampoon Radio Hour" instead of merely recycling sketches from the magazine for the air. He brought Gilda into the fold, and that was why, in August 1974, she took a train named, I believe, *The Samuel P. Marchbanks* from Toronto to New York to work on the "Lampoon" radio show and the second *Lampoon* stage show.

"Belushi makes me laugh like you can't imagine," Gilda used to say. "He's a mentor to me."

On more than one occasion Gilda recalled:

"I had worked with Belushi at Second City, so he knew my work, and I knew his. But I think the real reason Belushi hired me was that I'm a good laugher. He knew I'd be a good audience for him!"

When Gilda connected with the "Radio Hour," it was a seminal moment in the history of American comedy.

As Tony Hendra, former editor of the *National Lampoon*, recorded it:

"It was the most complete fusion yet of the *National Lampoon* crowd with the Second City alumni. John Belushi had taken control of the 'Radio Hour' and had tapped Gilda, Brian Murray [Bill's older brother], Harold Ramis, and Joe Flaherty to make a repertory company of extraordinary talent."

When Belushi took over the "Radio Hour," it had been losing money hand under fist. Belushi's great contribution from a business standpoint was assembling a repertory company that not only was talented but could also, due to its strong improvisational training, create live-to-tape humor in more-or-less real time. Previously, under the lead of nontheatrical, nonradio people like Michael O'Donoghue, the show had been very funny but far too labor-intensive. O'Donoghue's brilliantly crafted and lovingly polished bits might take two hundred man-hours of work to produce a three-minute piece. Belushi's rep company could improvise an hour of program in two or three hours of work. It was a vast economy of scale, and still the quality of the show stayed right up there with the *Lampoon* magazine and the *Lampoon*'s Broadway hit, *Lemmings*.

According to Hendra, the rep company also gave the radio show a group sense it had never had before. Its unique mix of Second City and *Lampoon* wit created a new kind of humor that would find its full expression in "Saturday Night Live."

For Gilda the "Radio Hour" was a chance to build on the fun she had had at WCBN in Ann Arbor. Her radio tap dancer had its conceptual counterpart in the "Camera Club of the Air." And the first of her zany news hens, Babwa Wawa, first lisped into being on the rarefied air of the "Radio Hour."

Gilda and Belushi enjoyed the "Radio Hour" very much. But the *Lampoon* brass pressed them and the rest of the troupe into service on another project whose aim was to recoup some of the hundreds of thousands of dollars the company had lost in radio production. This was called *The National Lampoon Show*, and it began as a traveling revue, touring college campuses in Canada and the Northeast.

The college students loved the show. It was especially a hit in Toronto, where Ivan Reitman, who was then producing a stage show called *The Magic Show*, caught it. Reitman hit it off with Matty Simmons, head of the *Lampoon*'s parent company, and together they decided to try out the "Lampoon Show" in New York.

The National Lampoon Show played at the New Palladium nightclub-theater in the Time-Life building. It got good reviews and was considered a worthy sequel to the huge satiric hit *Lemmings*. It also introduced a jaded New York to the fresh new wit of Gilda, Belushi, and a man called "The Honker," aka Bill Murray.

At the time, I was living in California. After Gilda moved back to the States, she encouraged me to try to "make it in New York," as she was doing.

Inspired by her success with the "Radio Hour" and *Lampoon Show*, and heartened by her invitation, I moved to Manhattan myself.

She met me at the airport, just as I had met her in Paris. But this time she was the hip old hand and I was the rube.

As we rode into Manhattan in a taxi, we caught up.

"I've been spending a year just looking for the sky," she said. "New York is really a weird place. You can't tell if it's the moon up there or just another streetlight. It's the only place in the world you can step out of a stretch limo right into a pile of steaming dogshit!"

It was the first time Gilda had lived in New York, but she had visited before, usually accompanied by Ellen. They had gone to see Ellen's father, a well-known journalist and former press secretary to the 1948 third-party presidential candidate Henry Wallace. Lou Frank was a charming, intelligent gentleman, and Gilda liked him very much.

"One day you'll write about how I got to know New York by coming here to visit your father," Gilda said to Ellen. Ellen has written some good things about Gilda, including her obituary in *The Nation*, entitled "A Death in the Family."

Having had some luck in publishing, I had also spent a fair amount of time in New York already, so the city did not faze me that much. But I had never lived there as part of the in-crowd, and Gilda was wondering how I was going to fit in.

"Let's see," she said. "You don't smoke anymore, right?"

"Right."

"And do you drink?"

"Well, hardly ever," I said.

"And do you eat meat?"

"Occasionally." I was California to the core at that time, an ex-hippie with a vengeance.

"Take drugs?"

"Not even aspirin."

"So?" she asked with a note of shocked wonderment in her voice. "What do you do for fun?"

For the next several months, while I was trying to find a permanent place to live, Gilda and I roomed together in her apartment on West Eighty-Fourth Street, just off Riverside Drive. It was a two-bedroom "parlor-floor-through" in a beautiful old stone house. The "parlor floor" is a New Yorkism, dating from the days when four-story brownstones housed whole families rather than just single investment bankers or TV stars. In those days the parlor was on what we would call, I guess, the mezzanine of the house. You walked up a flight of outside steps through the ornate front door into the front hall, turned right or left, and you were on the "parlor floor." Now that houses have been chopped into apartments, if you're lucky, as Gilda and I were, you have a "floor-through," which, if it's on the parlor floor, goes all the way through the house to the back garden. Usually the owner of the ground floor, not the parlor floor, controls access to the garden.

Gilda's entire living room was painted bright blue, one shade darker than sky, with white trim and a white marble fireplace. She had a big, shaggy white throw rug on the floor, which she later gave to me. She had imported a couple of rocking chairs from Pears Street, but the rest of the furniture belonged to the super-tenant, who was subletting it to her.

It seemed to me an odd color scheme, so overwhelmingly blue, but it was conducive to a certain headiness that, mixed with the smell of bubble gum, proved to be good for comedy and careers.

Belushi had hired Gilda to play "the girl" in the show.

Gilda delivered her first line in the overture-introduction, skidding out onto the stage on her knees with arms outspread and a big smile, belting out in bubbling tones:

"And there's a *girl* in the show!"

As always, Gilda derived her characters from her own life. Her signature character in the *Lampoon* show, Rhoda Tyler Moore, had come from her getting what she called "New Yorked" a number of times.

"God damn, I've just been New Yorked again" was the way she'd put it, when, for instance, she had been cheated and insulted by her taxi driver, stepped out of the cab only to be soaked by another cab driving full speed through a puddle, and then, on the sidewalk, stepped directly with her new shoes into that ever-present huge pile of dog duty.

Bill Murray describes the run this way:

"In New York we did the show to a really hostile crowd. They came to curse at the actors.

"Gilda was great. She did Rhoda Tyler Moore, playing a blind girl trying to make it in New York."

She set up the character by skipping onto the stage, swinging her cane, and singing her upbeat theme song:

> Who's always the last one in the room?
> The one who poked her eyes out with a broom;
> Who's the girl who likes everyone she meets
> 'Specially if they help her cross the streets. . . .

Bill Murray continues:

"John Belushi played her boyfriend, and he'd change his voice and pretend to be these thugs hitting her, beating her, cuffing her around on the stage. Then he'd change back to the boyfriend's voice and pretend to be saving her from the thugs. Then he'd pretend to be a big dog humping her, and then he'd chase the dog off. . . . It was really funny, and she'd die with this wonderful blind face, this wonderful smile. She'd run, with a cane, full speed into this wall. To get a laugh. She was covered with bruises. You had to admire her!"

Gilda and Belushi were a fantastic combination onstage. Her peppy innocence dovetailed marvelously with his amazing ability to be sympathetic one moment and sadistic the next.

Gilda loved Belushi dearly. The most telling thing she ever said about him was something she wrote as a caption on a large card she sent him once when he was in the hospital. The card was a picture of the two of them together in a touching pose. Belushi was clean-shaven, his thinning hair slicked back and sideburns long. He had his shirt off and was standing holding Gilda in a masterful embrace with his right arm. She had her hair long and bushy and was wearing jeans and a tank top, with her arms crossed against her breast. She was curling up in his arm with a sexy smile and a sultry look on her face, in a pose that looked like it had come out of *A Streetcar Named Desire.* Printed in balloon letters with Gilda's distinctive arrowheads, her caption read, with chillingly prophetic precision:

> In loving memory of John Belushi, who can hit me without hurting me and who can hurt me without hitting me.
>
> Gilda Susan

Belushi was never funnier than when he was in a kitchen.

One night Gilda and I went to a party in Washington

Square Mews. All the *Lampoon Show* people were there, plus a group of then-unknowns who are now more famous than God and twice as rich.

Belushi was hungry, as usual, and went to the refrigerator. Belushi rarely visited a house without cleaning out the refrigerator. Like Gilda, he was in love with food. As he turned with a sandwich in hand, he realized he was looking through a kind of proscenium arch into the living room. He suddenly began to improvise a cooking show.

"Remember," he said, in a Julia Child–like falsetto, "you cannot make an omelet without breaking eggs."

To ever-increasing peals of laughter he began to break eggs, many of them, one after another, into a saucepan. And then he began to add large quantities of butter, bread, cheese, cereal, milk, plums, horseradish, suet, fish flakes, vanilla extract, cornstarch, wine, ice cream, cake, and whatever else he could find in the pantry. He finally folded in heaping amounts of napkins, paper towels, and steel wool and topped it all with a dusting of Drāno.

Performed in Belushi's inimitable "talking samurai" style, it made the audience die with laughter. I was sitting next to Gilda, who was literally falling over on her back and waving her legs in the air.

Between gasping sobs of laughter, she stammered, "I'm p-p-peeing in my pants."

"I'm blessed to be surrounded by the funniest people in the world," she said later that night, when she had recovered her breath, wiped the tears from her face, and changed her underwear.

Lorne Michaels had discovered New York and the *National Lampoon* at about the same time Gilda had. Lorne went to see her again in the *Lampoon Show* and resolved then and there to sign her up for a new project he was trying to put over with NBC.

She polled all her friends the night she got Lorne's invitation to become the first cast member in this weird new live comedy experiment.

"Should I do it?" she asked. "Or should I take this other, much more secure offer from David Steinberg to work on a syndicated comedy talk show and revue based in Calgary?"

After all, she reasoned, she was already a big star in Canada, having done a number of shows on the CBC. She liked David Steinberg and did not really know Lorne. The Calgary thing was a real job, with a guaranteed income more than twice what Lorne could offer and a certain run, working five days a week. Who knew what would happen on this fledgling NBC tryout?

I told her she should definitely take the NBC job.

Gilda also solicited Lorne's advice.

"Should I wait?" Gilda asked Lorne, referring to the six months it was going to take before "Saturday Night" was to premiere. Lorne always claimed he named it that so the network could remember what night it was on.

"I don't know," Lorne answered. "I wouldn't say you have to. But yeah, I think you should."

Lorne was sure about Gilda, and he tried hard to convince her to give up the Steinberg offer. He had his agent, Bernie Brillstein, call Gilda to point out that her exposure on the worst disaster possible at NBC would still be considerably greater than on the greatest syndication hit in all of Canada.

Many of her other friends advised her to take the NBC job for exactly the same reason. There were no dissenting votes. To this day each one of them is certain he or she is the one who convinced Gilda to take the job.

"Gilda always loved to poll her friends," Lorne recalled about this moment. "She trusted them implicitly, and she usually did what they recommended. She somehow knew that they were really looking out for her best interests instead of their own. Gilda did that to people."

After getting approved by Lorne's corporate counterpart, Dick Ebersol, Gilda became the first Not Ready for Prime Time Player.

Her first official act was to tell her mother. Unfortunately, Detroit's NBC affiliate was virtually the only one in the country that, in 1975, did not pick up the show. So Gilda's conversation with her mother went like this:

"Hey, Mom, I just got this great job in New York on this national TV show, and it goes to every city in the world except Detroit."

Her mother replied:

"Gilda, why don't you get married?"

In a way she did—to her job. Gilda was never comfortable being all alone in anything. She immediately tried to draw her favorite performing partners, Dan Aykroyd, John Belushi, and Bill Murray, into the company. Lorne resisted all of them at first. Belushi scared him. He wasn't sure about Aykroyd. Murray already had another job as a member of the Prime Time Players on another show called, oddly enough, "Saturday Night Live with Howard Cosell." That was an arrogant and not very funny ABC show hosted by the arrogant and not always funny Howard Cosell. But soon enough Cosell was canceled and Gilda and Lorne saw eye to eye.

Gilda and the other cast members that first season got what she called "Mickey Rooney–Judy Garland deals." They were paid $750 a show during the first year, with gradual raises to $900 by the second. At first they averaged only three shows a month. The writers got $650 a week, rising to $700 by March of the first season. Since the writers were paid weekly, instead of by the show, Gilda thought they had the better deal.

As for Henrietta and Michael, for the first few months of the show they had to drive to Lansing on Saturday nights to see that their little Gilda was really on her way to becoming America's sweetheart.

Mickey was so proud of her he just about burst. But, according to Kitty, Henrietta could only find fault:

"She was so selfish. She spent all her time on herself. She didn't give Gilda anything, neither love nor time. Gilda never forgave her."

When I came to live with Gilda, I had to spend time trying to make some money myself. As I had helped advise Gilda on what job she should take, she did the same for me. It made a story Gilda was fond of retelling to anyone who asked her advice about how to get a job.

"You won't believe how my friend Dave got a job in New York," Gilda would say. "He just called up Mike Wallace and got hired at CBS News!"

It was true. I had had no intention of working for CBS or even going into broadcasting. At the time I was strictly a writer, a print journalist, and was trying to get something at the *New York Times.* But Gilda had advised me to leave no turn unstoned.

"You have to be methodical," she said. "Think of it like a military campaign."

So I had made a list of everyone I knew in New York, including my colleagues at the *New York Times.* My plan was to call each one and then to go see them one by one, asking each if he or she knew of any jobs. It was like hunting ducks with a shotgun. Something was likely to drop out of the sky if you just generally aimed in the right direction.

So even though I had met him just once before, in Ann

Arbor, Mike Wallace made my list. I figured what the hell—ain't got nothing, got nothing to lose.

Gilda and I were both twenty-nine years old at the time. How desperate, yet how hopeful, is youth. And how that hope is rewarded.

Gilda used to love to tell people what happened next. It proved that it is necessary only to be bold to obtain favors.

She was in her living room on Eighty-Fourth Street giving me moral support as, working my way down the list, I eventually took a deep breath and called Mike Wallace at CBS News. Believe it or not, he answered the phone himself. I recognized his famous voice and, nervous as a hummingbird, launched into a confused speech. But I succeeded in reminding him that we had met years ago in Ann Arbor and that he had said to me:

"Kid, if you ever get to New York, look me up!"

He could not have been more gracious. He invited me over to his office at CBS on West Fifty-Seventh Street later that very day. I was beside myself with excitement, and Gilda thought it was unbelievably funny.

Mercury must have been trining Saturn that day, or perhaps my moon was in the sign "Do Not Disturb." In any case, before seeing Mike, the same day I also had my dream appointment at the *New York Times.* It went better than I had any right to hope for. Walter Goodman, a member of the editorial board, offered me my choice of jobs. I could become an editor on the travel section or a writer in a new post, in Los Angeles, reporting on Hollywood.

God, was I a spoiled brat! I said to myself I had just come out from California, and I did not feel like going back to hated Los Angeles. (As it turns out, that job has become the albatross of *Times* reporters. But hey, Walter, if it's still open. . . .)

I was noncommittal and said I'd get back to them after I saw Mike Wallace. The look on their faces told me that

Commissioned by *Rags* magazine, photographer Carolyn Schultz spent three days with Gilda in 1977 capturing moments both playful and personal. This was one of Gilda's favorite photo sessions and her first appearance as a cover girl. Since her children's theater performances in Ann Arbor, Gilda had been captivated by the role of fairy princess, and she was so pleased with this photo that she used it to make her own postcards.

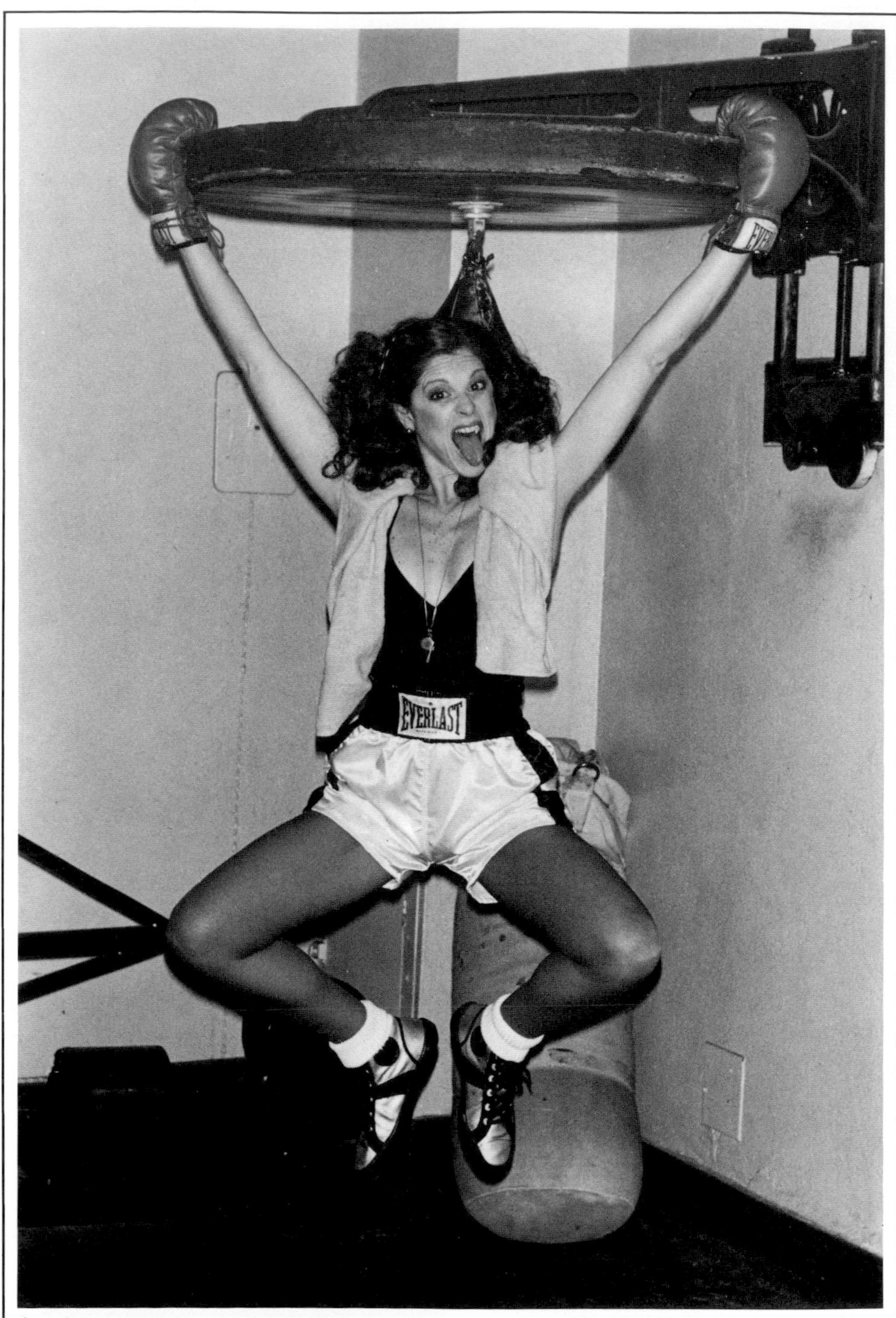
EVERLAST

EVERLAST

either I had just made a tremendous gaffe or as soon as I got a job with CBS all my friends from the *Times* would be calling me to see if there was anything for them.

In the taxi from Forty-Third Street over to Fifty-Seventh Street I prepared for my interview with Mike Wallace. On the back of an envelope I extemporaneously jotted down some story suggestions for "60 Minutes."

Mike did not hire me for "60 Minutes." But while I was in the room, he did call the news director of WCBS Radio, and he said:

"Got a great kid here, excellent writer, good on the air. Um-hm. Um-hm. OK, thanks."

He turned to me and said, "You've got an appointment tomorrow at ten o'clock."

The next day, when I went there, the radio executives fawned over me like I was the jeweled stoat of happiness.

"Mike Wallace called and said some very nice things about you," one gushed. "When can you start?"

As we had done for her a few weeks before, Gilda and I now discussed which job *I* should take.

How could I turn down the *New York Times*? I asked.

Gilda said:

"No, you asked Mike Wallace for a favor, and he did you one. Now you have to take it. How could you turn down a job Mike Wallace got for you?"

She was right. As she began her meteoric rise at NBC, I began a long and eventful career at CBS and the other networks.

In February 1977, when Gilda and I were still living together, an article I had written appeared on the front page of the Sunday *New York Times* travel section.

Gilda was very impressed, showing the piece to Bill Murray, John Belushi, and others.

I was surprised that she was so impressed by what,

to me, was nothing more than a typical earning of daily bread.

"No, Dave, this is no small thing," Gilda said admiringly.

Gilda was always very supportive of my writing efforts. She looked up to writers and for years felt it was something beyond her, something she did not have the patience and discipline to do.

I knew she could write, and finally I hit on how to break the ice for her. I told her there was no secret to writing.

"Just write the same way you talk," I said, and it was as if the scales fell from her eyes. She knew she could talk well and that her talking was effective communication. She began "writing" into a tape recorder almost at once.

"This is me, Gilda, writing in the way she really talks," she would say into the mike.

Even after she left "SNL," when she became a "professional writer," she still preferred to talk her books and articles onto tape, then have them transcribed. Verbal gems regularly fell from her lips. She spoke in poems.

In 1982 the editors of the *New York Times Magazine* asked me to write a profile of her.

"No, Dave, I don't think so," she said with a laugh.

She acted as if I was not really serious. I was because, as usual, I needed the money.

"I'm sorry, Dave. I don't want you to write it because you know me too well," she said, smiling.

I believed she was afraid I'd mention something about her throwing up—her bulimia was then not public knowledge—or about her love life. I told her I'd keep any secrets she wanted.

Again she said no.

"But don't worry," she added gently. "You'll write about me one day."

During our years together I always encouraged Gilda to

write, and she never stopped encouraging me to perform. She especially thought I should go on the air. I protested that nobody wanted to look at a guy they would suspect of being a Hasidic rabbi. She disagreed.

"Look at Joel Siegel. You could do what Joel Siegel does."

She mentioned Joel because he was chubby, wore glasses, had a mustache, was a friend of mine, and had recently interviewed her for one of his "Good Morning America" and "Eyewitness News" spots.

At the time Gilda made that suggestion, I was working with Joel at ABC as a writer/producer. Word had gradually gotten out that Gilda was a friend of mine. It was a little while after Gilda had invented Roseanne Roseannadanna; she was at the crest of her fame. One of the principal anchorwomen at "Eyewitness News" at the time was named Roseanne Scamardella. Most people in New York thought Gilda had at least heard that name and decided to use a variation of it for one of her "generic anchorwoman" characters.

For some reason Gilda at first felt very strange about admitting that the name Roseanne Scamardella had influenced her character's name. She had a strong fear of being accused of stealing material or not being original, and perhaps this contributed to it. Of course she was nothing but original. But she was afraid people might think she was somehow derivative, so she shied away from any identification with Roseanne Scamardella.

She may have been influenced by Lorne's policy of making sure the cast never even looked at material submitted by anyone but the show's writers, so as never to be exposed to a charge of plagiarism.

In any case, two different times people at "Eyewitness News" approached me with "ideas" for a "story" on the "relationship" between Gilda and Roseanne.

The first time it was proposed in a very strange way—through a young woman assistant on the staff, a friend of mine, who said she had been asked to speak to me by Roseanne. Roseanne was also a friend, but this appeared to me a blatant effort to let her bask in Gilda's light, and I refused.

"Gilda doesn't know Roseanne," I said. "There is no relationship."

She conveyed this information. A month or so later another emissary appeared with a similar request, this time from the big boss.

"What's the story?" I said. "There's no story."

"Well, you know—Gilda and Roseanne," the emissary said and made a proposal—with a twist:

They proposed to me that Gilda and Roseanne meet at a certain restaurant, La Terrasse on Shelter Island, and we do a "story" on their first meeting—maybe even a live remote, from the restaurant, on a beautiful summer weekend in the Hamptons.

Unfortunately, I had created the opening for this twist myself.

To help out two old friends of Gilda's and mine, Kitty and Eric Pergeaux, for the past few weeks I had strongly encouraged people at "Eyewitness News" and elsewhere to patronize their new restaurant, the selfsame La Terrasse, on lovely, peaceful, starfish-shaped Shelter Island in Peconic Bay. To entice their business I told them—truthfully, of course—that the owners were friends of Gilda's and all the Hampton high types ate there. Gilda indeed always ate there when she was on the island and had been present at the grand opening.

So some of the upper management of WABC-TV, being crazy to cash in on the cachet, notoriety, and utter coolness of "Saturday Night," had indeed visited the restaurant.

Instead of leaving big tips they hatched a plan to get some cheap publicity out of it—namely, the proposed "story."

I was divided.

Of course it was the sleaziest idea afoot in New York that day. But Kitty and Eric had been friends of mine as long as Gilda and were also old friends of hers. Kitty was the irrepressible Kitty Shannon of Toronto and Ann Arbor, and she and Gilda had been inseparable since college, as chronicled earlier. Kitty had married her college sweetheart, Eric Pergeaux, a self-defrocked French "count" who could drink prodigious quantities of wine and still go Windsurfing as if he were sober as an athlete. If there was any chance that the publicity might also profit Kitty and Eric, well—I thought Gilda might welcome the chance to help them. So I decided I would at least mention it to her this time.

She thought it over and at first indicated she might do it. But then, on reflection, she balked:

"No, Dave, I'm not gonna do it. I'd like to help Kitty and Eric. I mean, I'm the one that encouraged them to open the restaurant in the first place. But don't send Roseanne Scamardella! Don't send Roger Grimsby! I don't wanna meet those people. They're just gonna want something from me."

"What would Roger Grimsby want from you?" I asked. He was the principal anchorman at WABC-TV, a very well-known figure in New York for more than fifteen years. It seemed to me that he was wealthy, popular, and a cool dude to boot, and he didn't really need Gilda.

"Trust me," she said. "He'll want something from me."

So that Shelter Island adventure never came off. I tried harder to protect her from the horde.

I thought it was interesting that years later Gilda freely admitted she *had* been intrigued by Roseanne Scamardella's name and had then played with it using one of her old favorite songs, "The Name Game," to get the name Roseanne Roseannadanna. By then she had grown much wiser and had seen that it cost her nothing to tell the whole truth as quickly and cleanly as possible. That, after all, was the secret to her humor and her life.

Incidentally, it's been reported that Scamardella received a hefty salary raise because she had become "more identifiable" as a result of Gilda's name game. And it's indisputable that Roseanne Scamardella, news anchorwoman, has in real life said stuff on television like:

"Amid the rats, dead cats, garbage, and feces. . . ."

Hey, who wrote that? The things we do to get laughs, or higher "Q-ratings"!

Gilda remained intrigued by the idea of letting Kitty and Eric profit from her fame. She even felt obligated, since Kitty had asked her for a loan to help start the restaurant but Gilda had refused.

"I don't loan money to friends," Gilda had said firmly. "But I'll give you all the support you need."

So soon after the aborted Shelter Island caper she stole WABC's "idea" and made it pay off for Kitty and Eric.

All the talk shows had been pestering her to appear that year, and she had said no to everyone. Finally, though, she agreed to do "Good Morning America," on one condition: that they shoot the whole thing at La Terrasse. Naturally they agreed—this time without Roseanne Scamardella.

"Good Morning America" filmed Gilda crossing on the Shelter Island ferry. On the restaurant's lovely terrace they interviewed her as she was eating an enormous bowl of mussels *marinière*, made with cream and shallots. Gilda ate with gusto during the entire interview, and she made sure Kitty was right beside her and appeared in all the shots.

The *New York Times* also "discovered" La Terrasse and

gave it two stars. Kitty and Eric had full houses for the rest of that season and the next two as well.

During this period Gilda and I both moved, so we lived around the corner from each other in Greenwich Village. Belushi lived right in between, in a cavernous walk-up flat at 376 Bleecker Street. Belushi's wife, childhood sweetheart Judy Jacklin, loved to call Gilda on the telephone. While chatting once, Judy suddenly said, "Just a minute!" as if she had left the water running in the kitchen and was going to turn it off.

Without hanging up, Judy ran full-speed to Gilda's house, half a block away. Judy had a key and appeared magically in Gilda's living room while, hapless as Lisa Loopner, Gilda was still waiting patiently for her to return to the other end of the telephone.

Gilda, of course, cracked up.

It was a living example of Gilda's theory of comedy: "Comedy is just truth, only faster!"

Gilda watched all kinds of television as "research" for her job. She especially felt duty-bound to watch NBC and often got a real pang of patriotism when she saw the NBC peacock unfold its tail on the screen.

"I'm in love with my logo!" she exclaimed on one such occasion.

When she could take her preference, she liked to watch movies and news. She has said that she developed her parody of reporters in reaction to "all those women reporting the news on TV. They always look like they're so frightened to lose their job. You know they're saying, 'We're women and we have credibility, we're journalists, we have no dicks, we don't go number two, we don't fart.' They're like, boss twatty perfect."

It was in their imperfections that Gilda was able to find

a foothold on their shoulders. Gilda's first anchorwoman parody, her priceless rendition of "Babwa Wawa," took shape not because Gilda had studied her but because she used to ask other people:

"OK, now, tell me—what does Barbara Walters do?"

She saw what made her stand out for other people, took those qualities, and twisted them one more turn of the screw, and Babwa Wawa was born.

Barbara Walters claimed she had never seen Gilda on television. In any case, in November of 1976 they met at a cocktail party at the Canadian consulate, in the Exxon building on Sixth Avenue in New York.

Even aside from their meeting, the party was a major historical event. Margaret Trudeau, the prime minister's wife, was there to present the official Canadian gift to the United States of America on the occasion of the American Bicentennial. And real history was made later, when Mrs. Trudeau left the party with Harry Belafonte, whom nobody could remember having invited. Later that night, at another party, she would meet, for the first time, the Rolling Stones and the illustrious Ron Wood.

At that second party Ron turned to Margaret and said: "So. What do you do with your time?"

She replied: "Well, I'm trying to get into photojournalism. . . ."

"Listen," he said. "We're doing a concert in Toronto in a couple of months. Why don't you come by the hotel?"

She did, and their torrid affair rocked the Canadian government with the year's juiciest scandal.

Meanwhile, back at the consulate. . . . At that time "Saturday Night" was still a rather underground phenomenon. The members of the cast were not yet household names, except in certain households where intoxicating substances were not rationed.

The senior Canadian diplomats had invited their favorite august Americans, including Walter Cronkite and Barbara Walters, to the reception.

However, there was one young diplomat, a Mr. F. David Smith, who barely knew anyone in New York except his wife Suzan's "cousin," this nutty actress named Gilda Radner who had been a big star in Canada while the Smith family had been posted in West Africa. Suzan, you recall, had always thought she was related to Gilda because Gilda used to spend weekends at her real cousin Judy's house, to avoid Henrietta.

*Any*ways, as Canadians would say, Smith and his wife invited Gilda and these as-yet little-known Canadian outlaws named Dan Aykroyd and Lorne Michaels to the party. Gilda was very excited about going. It was her first "embassy affair" and would be the first time she had ever seen Barbara Walters in person. When she came, she brought Laraine Newman, Anne Beatts, Rosie Shuster, and some other cast members with her.

The dignitaries were dressed to kill in formal wear, strictly black tie. But the "SNL" people had all just popped over from rehearsal at Rockefeller Center and were in their typical bohemian dungarees and tennis shoes.

"They looked like hippie rejects," Smith recalls.

Gilda was the best dressed of all the players, wearing a skirt with a velvet blazer and boots.

In his best baritone Walter Cronkite commented on the motley crew:

"I'm interested to see all the 'Saturday Night' people here," he said to Smith. "I understand they're real renegades."

"They're mostly Canadians," Smith said proudly, lying for queen and country.

Cronkite chuckled and said:

"Leave it to Canadians to be so iconoclastic."

Smith was outwardly pleased by the compliment. But inwardly he was saying, "Eh? Eh?" He found it hard to credit as iconoclasm the cultural sensibility whose greatest achievement, in his opinion, was producing the cleanest beavers in the world. (Later, seeing the error of his ways, he began sending back dispatches to Ottawa recommending a politics of "eco-roading," but that's for another history.)

Early in the party, Gilda buttonholed Smith, grabbing him by the arm.

"You have to introduce me to Barbara Walters," Gilda insisted. "I've never met her."

David took her over to where Barbara was holding court in her cocktail dress. She was also wearing boots.

"Barbara, I'd like you to meet Gilda Radner," Smith said.

Barbara had an extremely blank look on her face. Plainly, she did not recognize the name.

Gilda said, in a very charming, cute, and self-effacing manner:

"Hi, I'm Gilda Radner. I'm the girl that does you on TV. I do an imitation of you on 'Saturday Night.' "

Barbara was unimpressed.

"Oh, really," she said. "Frankly, I've never seen it."

Gilda became very flustered. As ever, her heart jumped right off her tongue.

"I've always admired you . . . I've been very nervous about meeting you . . . I just do the sketch for fun . . . I've been worried you might be offended . . ."

Barbara then shifted into bruising speed:

"Oh, *yeah*, that's right. Someone told me about that, that someone did an imitation of me."

Suddenly drawing Gilda into a corner of the room, away from a gathering crowd, Barbara continued:

"Er. . . exactly what is it you do? Do it for me right now!"

Knees shaking, Gilda proceeded to do her imitation.

Barbara did not react well at first.

"Uh-huh. Uh-huh. I don't see what's so funny about that," she snapped.

When Gilda had finished, Barbara said:

"So? That's it?"

Gilda nodded.

Barbara took a deep breath, and then her curiosity prevailed. Her voice changed octaves:

"Tell me how you do it," Barbara asked.

Gilda explained to her: "You're easy to do. I just change the *l*s and *r*s to *w*s. Like this: 'Hewwo, I'm Babwa Wawa at Wawge.' "

Barbara finally gave a little laugh and said:

"Yeah, I'm working on my *ehw*s and *ahw*s."

Although she had finally managed to get a laugh, Gilda was very upset by this incident, worried that she had been thoughtlessly cruel. Excusing herself from Barbara, she immediately went to the ladies' room for an indecently long time.

After that meeting Gilda became a little concerned that she might have seriously damaged Barbara Walters's credibility:

"The other day I watched the news and realized I could really be hurting her," she said on one occasion. "I know that there is a contingent of listeners out there that can hear only her speech impediment because of me. I think, God, what have I done? She's just this teeny-tiny little slip of a thing. But tough as an old tit!" She laughed. "Well, she's on top of everything. I guess she's tough enough to survive."

Nevertheless, Smith, the former consul, says he has hated Barbara Walters ever since this episode and cannot bear to watch her on television.

"Gilda and the others were so young and unworldly back then," he remembers. "Gilda was trying so hard to be kind. Barbara Walters did not have to be so cold, so rude to her."

It was one of the few times Gilda, with her winning way, did not bring out the best in people.

Just off her gig as "the girl in the show," about two months after she took the "Saturday Night" job, Gilda began to become aware of the macho machinations of big-time humor. As Michael O'Donoghue told journalists, "It does help when writing humor to have a big hunk of meat between the legs, I find. . . ."

In the fall of the first season of "SNL," a note went up on a bulletin board in the "Saturday Night" offices on the seventeenth floor of 30 Rockefeller Plaza. All the women on the show were invited to a slumber party at Anne Beatts's apartment. Potato chips and Tab were on the menu. The agenda was how to keep Belushi, Aykroyd, Chase, and their running dogs and lickspittle lackeys from dominating the women on "Saturday Night."

According to the detailed account in the history *Saturday Night*, by Doug Hill and Jeff Weingrad, Marilyn Suzanne Miller had the floor first. Gilda had once introduced Marilyn to me by saying "Her mother writes the dictionary." Marilyn, daughter of the chief lexicographer of the *Random House Dictionary*, is one of the most talented comedy writers in the country and had the most television experience of any woman on the show. She opined that male chauvinism was probably inevitable on "SNL." Perhaps, she added, taking a cue from Tex Antoine, the women should just lie back and enjoy it.

Anne Beatts agreed that some form of phallicism was probably inescapable. She said the *National Lampoon* had been the same way, having started at an all-male school like Harvard. She had been the only woman editor, which she likened to "being a black voter in the South: everyone else had to spell *cat*, and you had to say when the Edict of Nantes was revoked."

Beatts also pointed out that it could be worse. Monty Python, for instance, had no women at all in the troupe. Women's parts were played by men in drag.

According to Hill and Weingrad, all the women agreed that the hardest time was on Monday afternoon, when the staff would pitch new ideas to Lorne. The men had louder voices, for one thing. For another, no one presented ideas more forcefully than Dan Aykroyd or Chevy Chase. Too often the women's ideas were lost when "the men wrote sketches where people got dressed up in suits of armor and banged into each other and fell down," as Anne Beatts put it. "The women just weren't attracted to that kind of humor."

Gilda agreed with Beatts that the men tended to divide humor into "hard" and "soft" comedy, "as if it were rectal tissue," according to Hill and Weingrad. And the end result was that the women got the worst parts, often as wallpaper girlfriends, secretaries, or receptionists, with lines in the nature of "Mr. Jones will see you now."

The estimable "girls" did not know at that time that among the funniest of their own sketches would be one where Gilda and the rest sat around discussing their periods.

Anyway, Gilda disagreed with Anne that an organized cadre was the best way to fight capitalist piggishness. Still not wanting to be overtly "political," Gilda said she frankly did not relish being branded a "hairy-legged dyke feminist."

She was afraid a rebellion would alienate the men even more. On top of it all, Gilda felt the women—or at least she—had an ally in Lorne.

The slumber party broke up early, and no one slept over, even though some had arrived in their pajamas. The girls finally agreed with Gilda's position that the best political and comedic course was just to be so funny they could not be ignored. Beatts, Shuster, and Miller resolved to write more material for the women, to make sure they had good stuff to do in every show. They upheld that resolution in sterling fashion over the next five years.

The spirit of the slumber party awakened many times, usually at the end of writers' meetings. Gilda, carrying the flag, would pipe up bravely:

"Hey, Lorne, are the girls going to be doing anything this week, or what?"

One of the things that grew directly out of that evening—and for Gilda harked back to Indian River, Michigan—was a sketch called "Slumber Party." Marilyn Miller wrote it, and all "the girls" participated along with the guest host, Madeline Kahn. The conceit of the sketch was that Madeline was filling the girls in on the authentic method of having sex. As had actually been the case at Liggett slumber parties, none of them had ever heard of anything so disgusting.

Madeline whispered:

". . . in you and then you scream and then he screams and then it's over." There was a moment of shocked, horrified silence. Laraine made a vomiting sound and pulled the blankets over her head.

With a stunned look on her face, Gilda said, in a flat voice full of horror:

"You lie, Madeline."

Unlike the above-mentioned feminist revolt, the central

political plan of the "SNL" troupe went askew. Like good sixties radicals, The Not Ready for Prime Time Players aspired from the beginning to "equality of opportunity," but not very successfully. Chevy Chase dominated "Saturday Night" during the show's first season. After he left to pursue a career in the movies, in October 1976, John Belushi bubbled up and came to the fore. After Belushi also defected to Hollywood, in 1979, Gilda became the first among equals, mainly for her original repertoire of wacky characters.

As Diane Rosen observed in *TV Guide*:

"When Gilda Radner arches her back to play Baba Wawa or wrinkles her nose under Emily Litella's bifocals to read her confused editorial replies to matters as pressing as 'Soviet Jewelry' and 'Violins on Television,' or cracks her gum as co-ed Rhonda Weiss, she is parading a cast of characters almost as familiar to the public as Lily Tomlin's Ernestine and Edith Ann."

With all due respect to Lily, the reporter could have gone on to name a veritable slumber party of others: the hyperkinetic, prepubescent, panty-showing Brownie Judy Miller; the gross, wiseacring news hen Roseanne Roseannadanna with her notorious armpit hair and eye gook; the sadomasochistic razor-tongued punk rocker Candy Slice; her daffy re-creation of Lucille Ball's Lucy Ricardo; Debbie Doody, Howdy's wife, a part considered certain death by other comedians; and the sniffling teenage nerd Lisa Loopner, who was so funny you forgot to laugh.

It was for this incredible range and brilliance that the National Academy of Television Arts and Sciences awarded Gilda an Emmy in 1978 for "outstanding continuing performance by a supporting actress in music or variety."

In spite of her undoubted talent and the indisputable

love of her audiences and co-workers, Gilda never sought the position of "lead player" on the show. Among other things, she was always acutely aware of her need to work as part of a team. She had tremendous respect for teammates like Marilyn Suzanne Miller, who tried to use in her writing every word her mother ever taught her. Marilyn also went to the University of Michigan, although she and Gilda did not know each other there. Gilda tried to fix Marilyn up with Justin Friedland, another Ann Arbor classmate who is now a senior producer for ABC News. It didn't work out. She tried to fix her up with Joel Siegel, with the same nonresults. Once I paid a visit to Charles Street when Marilyn was there. I believe Gilda set the whole thing up, because she seemed to be angling for Marilyn and me to get together. Marilyn was sexy, smart, and incredibly funny, and she was wearing tight jeans and sexy high boots. But I missed out on a good thing and went for some bimbo instead.

After they had somehow picked up the vibe that I was not going to make a play for Marilyn, her eyes met Gilda's. With a wry look on her face, Marilyn suggested a sketch idea.

"How about 'Smart Girls'? What do you think? How they never get the guy?"

Gilda thought it had possibilities. They began working on it right on the spot. But they soon gave up after it began to seem too pathetic.

One of Marilyn's best creations was the "Periods" sketch mentioned earlier. It went something like this:

Gilda is opening presents. The other girls are gathered around.

"Oh, look—a melon baller!"

"I feel terrible. I'm about to get my period."

"Me too. Mine's here now."

"What's this?"

"It's a match lighter."

"Oh, thanks, that's just great."

"Yeah, I'm just getting over mine."

"Yeah, that's even worse, when you're just getting over it."

"Yeah, and even the whole next week I feel terrible."

"Right. And the week before it comes is even worse."

"And I can't stand it when I'm ovulating, right between periods. That's probably the worst of all."

"Look, a nose-hair clipper. . . ."

For three seasons the women performers—Gilda, Jane Curtin, and Laraine Newman—shared a dressing room.

"It was tiny," Jane recalled, "but there were times when that was the only place to go to get any sort of peace. Gilda was doing a lot of interviews, and the only place she could go was in our dressing room. Laraine and I would sit there in that very, very small room and act nonchalant."

Laraine confessed to *People* magazine: "I was terribly jealous of Gilda. Terribly. I knew she'd earned it. The audience loved her. But it hurt so much."

Gilda used to joke that when the show finally ended, the three of them would split a gold watch.

7

Splendors and Miseries of "Saturday Night"

"Saturday night became this national phenomenon"

JUST BEFORE, DURING, AND AFTER THE "SATURDAY NIGHT" era, Gilda and I were particularly close, reminiscent of our old days in Ann Arbor. We felt we could really talk to each other, without any of the posturing or manipulating that characterizes life in New York in the late twentieth century, especially in our chosen field of "the media."

She frequently invited me to "Saturday Night" during the five years she was with the show.

I hardly need mention that it was a fabulous, unparalleled scene, wittier than the Algonquin Round Table, more bohemian than Paris in the twenties, and just as grand as the Belle Epoque.

Like the Belle Epoque, the "Saturday Night Live" milieu was a dazzling mirage that has never really been captured on film or in print. The history *Saturday Night*, by Doug Hill and Jeff Weingrad, is a detailed, meticulously researched piece of work that faithfully records all the ups and downs of the show. I have not hesitated to use its information when necessary in this account. However,

Gilda refused to be interviewed for that book or any other, so the information on her is quite slim (as she always wanted to be). But otherwise their book is so detailed, so conscientiously impartial, that in spite of its excellence as journalism it seems in some way to miss the essential spirit of the whole epoch.

As Gilda said, "It wasn't only us. The Travolta movie *Saturday Night Fever* was out too. Saturday night became this, this national phenomenon!"

Like the Belle Epoque's nostalgic mix of the frivolous *monde* and naughty *demimonde*, bathed in a Proustian chiaroscuro of salon life and scandalous love, "Saturday Night" was a freewheeling blend of the sacred, the brilliant, and the profane, an international salon of the highest caliber as well as a sex-and-drugs-and-rock-and-roll empire that redefined art, culture, fashion, and especially humor.

The Belle Epoque is associated with Paris at its wickedest and most frolicsome—the era of the Moulin Rouge and Maxim's, where Russian grand dukes drank champagne out of the slippers of feather-bedecked cocottes.

Likewise, "Saturday Night" is associated with New York at its most decadent—the era of Studio 54, Trax, and the Limelight, where rock stars drank champagne strained through the edible panties of charmingly beautiful adventuresses in red silk dresses.

In the last century, to the strains of Offenbach, the wealthy and privileged waltzed from balls to receptions, from spas to châteaus, from yachts to gilded carriages.

In our time, to the strains of Paul Simon, the elite boogied from all-white parties in Amagansett to the Shelter Island Beach Club to yachts and gilded Cadillacs in Bel Air. The two centuries almost blend into one, the men elegant and mustachioed, the women lovely in rustling ruffles and beautiful tennis whites often dripping with pearls and diamonds.

Europe in the Belle Epoque was like one vast kingdom, where emperors, kings, and princes vied with one another for splendor and opulence at their royal courts.

"Saturday Night" likewise was dominated by princes from Chevy to Belushi to Lorne to Mick Jagger, who all vied with one another for splendor in the eyes of television viewers and rock fans. Like royalty, Belushi, in the period we are speaking of, might react in shocked surprise or worse if anyone outside his trusted inner circle spoke to him or, God forbid, touched him.

In this scene Gilda was always queen of the room, totally comfortable and kind in her fairy princess persona. And she had the awesome, truly queenly power of making everyone feel her equal.

Like the "Saturday Night" period, the Belle Epoque was a golden age for arts and music. As did the operas of Massenet and Ravel in those days, in this era television became an essential part of daily life. Belushi's, Bill Murray's, and Gilda's expressions entered the language: "But noooooo," "Get out of here, you knucklehead, I really mean it," "Never mind," "It's always something," and so on.

Balloons and bicycles, autos and airplanes changed forever the way people spent their leisure and led to great booms in travel and exploration during the Belle Epoque. Television served the same function in the seventies.

Studio 54, in this epoch, was the most exclusive two thousand square feet on the face of the earth.

One night in 1978 it became exclusive cubed. Even the crème de la crème waited jealously in the street while the place closed for a "Saturday Night Live" private party. Isa, my fiancée, and I were fortunate enough to be on Gilda's list, and we prepared for one of those nights that last eight days.

As you entered Studio 54, you became aware of the scent of roses. Their petals were strewn everywhere.

The music was nothing short of astounding. That night, at Studio 54, was the world premiere of the "I Love New York" theme song. It became so wildly popular all over the world that it is now trite. But the first time it was ever played, *in* New York, at the Studio 54 "Saturday Night" party—the house went wild.

Baryshnikov was there, dancing with Margaux Hemingway. My future wife, the finest dancer in Brazil, was there. Gilda's hair was flowing down as she let it rip on the dance floor, and she was wearing her favorite salmon-pink jumpsuit.

The best free bar in the Western Hemisphere was sluicing rivers of alcohol. Great food in vast quantities groaned to be eaten.

There was an upstairs, also strewn with flower petals, where Belushi was hanging out. I take the Fifth on what sort of activities were occurring there. Suffice it to say it was the badass crowd: Meat Loaf, Paul Shaffer, an excellent bunch, with their customary carfuls of beautiful women, interesting friends, and esoteric toys.

There was also a liberal quantity of what Gilda used to call "the devil's dandruff," served in buckets, with a dipper.

More than anything, there was a special feeling, a special glow, golden twinkles in the air. The atmosphere was as rare as it gets. Unless you were an experienced climber, you needed oxygen at that height. Nobody there would have traded places with anyone else in the world that night.

In fact there *was* no one else in the world that night. As human society goes, it was the pinnacle of the universe, a planet of its very own, in its own perfect orbit. These advanced beings had no desire for contact with lesser civilizations.

At first Gilda had a hard time getting used to her universal fame. She would say:

"I can't understand how I got famous. It seemed like I just kept taking the next job, and it turned out that millions of people were suddenly watching me do it. The first time I ever saw the word *famous* it was on a menu in Detroit, where they said, 'Famous chili.' Is that how famous I am?"

"We were very insulated that first year," Gilda recalled to a reporter. "The press mostly focused on Chevy, and the rest of us weren't confronted with a flash of fame."

She did not really realize how famous she was getting until the second season of the show, when the cast was invited to Houston for the opening of a shopping center. Twenty-five thousand people showed up.

"We went onstage," Gilda recalled, "and suddenly there were these thousands of people screaming our names. Laraine and I both started to cry. It was like being a rock star. It was like being a bride."

Gilda had a running gag about why she took the "Saturday Night" job:

"Now I don't have to make up excuses for not having a date. I'm working every Saturday night!"

Indeed, she was working very, very hard, and she did not have many dates. She was always sure that guys were intimidated by her fame.

"They think, Oh, she's famous. She can go out with anyone she wants. She's probably fucking Jack Nicholson tonight. So I end up prowling the streets for food alone at three o'clock in the morning."

On the other side of that coin, she soon got over her befuddlement at finding herself famous and began to realize that her tireless efforts deserved the recognition she was getting.

"I worked hard for this, Dave. You know that, but a lot of people don't, and they resent me. When you're famous, your whole life comes back on you, like a bad dinner or something. All of these people from your past show up just to say hello. That's sort of frightening. Because there are some parts of your life that you don't always want to remember. . . .

"But when you become a star—you know why they call it a star? Because everything starts revolving around you, like the planets around the sun. It's like going into orbit. I could really be a bitch if I wanted to, you know. I could make everyone squirm. I know I could. But it's not my nature. . . ."

She really did not have it in her to be mean, nasty, or bitchy to anyone. The most she would do is vanish, like the fairy princess.

"I am almost always working," she once told an interviewer. "Woody Allen once said it was impossible for him to take a vacation—he said he could never 'vacate'—and neither can I. It's not that I do it consciously, but I'm always absorbing what's going on around me through a comic lens. People's mannerisms, the way they walk . . . these things never escape me. It's not that I'm thinking all the time. I feel I should try to be, because that seems like real, grown-up work. But I'm not a writer or a creator. I'm an actress—and, though I'm smart, I'm not very analytical.

Even when I'm working, in a certain kind of way I'm relaxed."

Her fans loved her deeply, and she loved them in return. But, as she said, "Sometimes you get really busy, really frazzled in New York, and you forget your manners." She admitted in an interview she was as guilty of this as her fans:

"I've had people get mad at me when they see me on the street," she said.

"Like, 'What are you doing out here?' They're going, like, 'Oh, a star,' but with resentment. Kids come screaming after me down the street, and I tend to forget—you know, I'm on my way home or just going for cigarettes, just doing my life. And they all want autographs, and I say, 'Isn't it enough that you *saw* me?' I mean, I'm ambitious, I'm greedy for attention . . . but isn't it enough that they *saw* me?"

In spite of that attitude, she was also the first to admit that she herself was just as star-struck as her fans.

"I saw Woody Allen at a party, and I couldn't stand it because he was just standing there, not talking to anybody, and I don't know him, but I love what he does so much, and I went up to him and *pushed him in the chest.*

"And it was awful. Because he didn't like it. He didn't say anything. And I said to people who knew him, 'Please, tell him I was just. . . .' And he probably—the terrible thing is, he probably didn't even notice. You know what I mean?"

One thing she unquestionably loved about having fans was getting fan mail. At first it came in at the rate of about one letter a day. Then it grew to dozens a day, then hundreds.

"One girl writes every week and tells me about her cat," she said with a laugh. "Guys mail pictures of themselves and say stuff like 'I want to lose my virginity to you.' I get a lot of dirty poems too," she said with a smile of wicked delight.

Sometimes she strained for romantic love from her fans and got love of comedy instead.

"One morning I changed clothes eight hundred times. I really did. I really wanted to look attractive. I really wanted to look sexy. And I went out, and a guy went by in a truck and leaned out and yelled, 'Hey, you're funny.' "

Once Gilda was walking down the street with Roy Blount, the writer, walking her peculiar gait that Roy has excellently described as a "tip-tip-tip . . . tip-tip . . . tip-tip-tip . . . teeter-wobbling fool's-progress manner."

"I have a very uncertain walk," she admitted. "But that's all right. So does my brother."

Anyway, a guy comes up behind her and says:

"Hey, Gilda, why do you walk funny?"

"Hey, you walk pretty funny yourself," she says back to this guy.

"Yeah," he says, "I'm in the *Guinness Book of World Records* for it. I walked like this all the way from Hartford." And he walks off, in a funny manner, into the distance.

"Hey," she says to Roy, always appreciative of a good crack, "that wasn't bad."

Roy reported all this in a charming piece he wrote about Gilda. She liked it very much and called him up to tell him that when she read it she fell down on the floor and sobbed, it was so *her*.

She tried to enjoy her celebrity, but she was continually feeling besieged. Once she told me she had been "taking a dump in a public bathroom, and I come out of my stall and find this really eager, smiling woman waiting for me who grabs me by the arm and whispers intimately, 'I love your work!' "

Gilda's work, as well as that of her cohorts on "Saturday Night," was happening all the time, all around her. Many of their funniest bits grew out of impromptu collaborations like the following:

One day Gilda and Belushi were improvising in Gilda's living room. I was there, so I became their foil.

"Dave is very good at languages," Gilda said to John. "He can learn any language in three months."

"That's nothing," John said. "I can teach you any language in a few minutes."

"Oh, really," Gilda said, knowing setup lines when she heard them. "How?"

"The same way you teach a parrot to talk," John said. "Repetition. For instance, in Albanian, the word for *hot soup* is *aashah*. Repeat after me: *aashah*."

He pronounced it in some impossibly ridiculous way, although I would be willing to bet it was authentic Albanian.

Gilda tried to imitate:

"Aash. Uh-shuh."

"No, no. 'Aashah.' Hot soup is *aashah*."

"I don't quite get it, Dr. Belush. Explain better. For instance, what's the word for *cold soup*?"

Belushi looked nonplussed for a moment. But then he replied:

"You never say 'cold soup.' Albanians like their soup hot!"

"OK," Gilda said. "Let's try something else. How do you say *horse*?"

"My God, Gilda, try to have a sense of proportion! Don't think about such a huge animal."

"OK, how about *ant*?"

"Too small. Don't annoy me with small stuff like that."

I chimed in. "OK, how about *goat*?"

Belushi fixed me with his famous beady little eyes.

"I'm sure the Albanians *have* a word for *goat*," he said testily. "But I wasn't there long enough to find out. I left just as the kids were being born, so they hadn't been named yet!"

This went on for an hour. One important variation involved teaching a parakeet to talk:

GILDA: Hello.
BELUSHI: Tweet.
GILDA: Hello.
BELUSHI: Tweet.
GILDA: (*Very deliberately*) Hel-lo.
BELUSHI: Tweet.
GILDA: Hel-ll-lo.
BELUSHI: Tweet.
GILDA: Hel-peep-lo.
BELUSHI: Tweet.
GILDA: Hel-peep.
BELUSHI: Tweet.
GILDA: Peep-peep.
BELUSHI: Tweet.
GILDA: Peep-tweet.
BELUSHI: Tweet.
GILDA: Tweet.

Eventually a beautifully honed version of this idea showed up as the very first sketch on the very first "Saturday Night." It was a classic featuring Belushi and Michael O'Donoghue. Belushi played a foreigner who speaks no English. O'Donoghue was teaching him useful English phrases, such as:

"I would like . . . to feed your fingertips . . . to the wolverines!"

Gilda often, as she has herself said, "laughed till I peed

in my pants and tears rolled out of my eyes" at the antics of "the guys," with special reference to Belushi.

In this Gilda differed greatly from other comedians. Most professional jokesters are incredibly egocentric and cannot stand it if another gets a laugh. Even Johnny Carson was like this for many years, although, now secure and mellow on Mt. Olympus, he has become more generous in his old age. But Gilda always gave as good a laugh as she got.

Thanks to her father, Gilda had great appreciation for all aspects of show business. God bless her, she had a special weakness for a lifelong semiprofessional art of mine: magic.

With great trepidation, more than once I performed my magic act for the "Saturday Night" cast and writers, at Gilda's charming two-story apartment on Charles Street. With the exception of Al Franken, they were all big fans of magic.

Belushi especially loved magic, and he was a perfect foil for it. His innate goodness emerged, and his love of spectacle knew no bounds. He became just like a little kid again. One night he volunteered to help me teach the audience a trick.

First I showed the trick to all: with my right side toward the audience, a red sponge the size and shape of a billiard ball vanished from my left palm and reappeared at my left elbow.

Belushi said, with his patented humorous sneer: "Aw, I know how you did that. It's in your other hand. You switched it."

"Thank you, sir. So, would you care to assist me in revealing exactly how this trick is done?"

"Sure," he smirked and came off the couch to sit in one of Gilda's straight-backed chairs, to my right, facing the rest of the audience.

I turned 180 degrees, so now my left shoulder faced the audience and they could see the back of my hands instead of the front. I did the trick again, very slowly, right in front of Belushi's prominent nose and bulging, miss-nothing eyes beneath those famous bushy eyebrows that seemed to have independent consciousness. This time, though, the audience could see "behind the scenes" at what was really happening in my hands. As Belushi had said, the ball *was* in my other hand. The audience—Gilda, Bill Murray, Tom Schiller, and Al Franken—could see it, nestled secretly in the crotch of my thumb. Belushi just saw an empty hand with fingers spread.

Belushi was puzzled, but the audience, except for Franken, laughed.

Now came the zinger.

"Now watch this," I said. "The ball appears again from my elbow. I take it in this hand, put it into this hand. Now I just tap the hand holding the ball . . . gently, one, two, three times . . . and the ball has totally disappeared!"

As I was saying this, in full view of the audience, on the word *three* I flung the ball over Belushi's head. It was done in such a way that, because of twenty-five years of practice, he could not see it. But to the audience it was a broad piece of business, so broad it was almost impossible to believe the volunteer could not know what was going on literally right under his nose and over his head.

I very slowly and with no extra motion showed John my unquestionably empty two hands, front and back. He shook his head in utter amazement.

He was still staring intently at my two hands, certain that the ball had to be in one or possibly both of them. The audience, except Franken, broke up with laughter. Gilda exclaimed:

"Naww, Dave, I don't believe it."

"Where'd it go?" Belushi demanded in a voice that left no doubt he was genuinely baffled.

I took another ball.

"Let's try it again," I said.

Again, with the audience able to see exactly what was happening, I ever so slowly made the ball vanish before Belushi's eyes, then threw it over his head, this time in a high arc.

The audience howled—except for Franken, who nodded.

I again showed Belushi my unmistakably empty hands. With a motion like a bull who has just been hornswoggled by a matador's veronica, Belushi shook his head hard, in true befuddlement. The audience, Franken excepted, roared with laughter.

For the third time I took up a sponge ball and made it disappear, again throwing it over Belushi's bewildered head. This time the audience collapsed in laughter, and even Franken, looking intently through his heavy glasses, let the corners of his thick lips curl upward a sixteenth of an inch.

Belushi could stand it no longer.

"*Where are those bucking falls*??!" he demanded in his best samurai spoonerism style, bringing down the house.

As I directed his gaze over his head and behind him, the audience applauded, and when Belushi perceived what had happened, he joined in, clapping and laughing like a baby loon.

That man really loved magic.

Afterward I spoke to Franken. I was extremely curious. I had always considered that trick audience-proof. It had been laying them in the aisles for many years; yet today, for the first time, someone had not laughed.

"How come you didn't laugh at the sponge ball trick?" I asked.

"Didn't think it was funny," Franken replied in his authoritative baritone honk.

Gilda was listening to this exchange. She, as usual, had enjoyed the show immensely.

"Just like a comedy writer," she said. "They never laugh at anything unless they've written it themselves."

Magic shows became one of the pet private entertainments of the "SNL" troupe, although it was extremely rare to actually put a magician on the show. Gilda proposed once that I come on, as "The Great Saltini," but Lorne demurred. According to Gilda, Lorne had booked a magician once, "The Great What's-His-Name," who was a disaster. He never wanted to pick another card again as long as he lived. And it is a fact that most magic *is* dreadful on television.

When I performed at Gilda's house it was a completely different story. It became drawing-room cabaret night. Perhaps I would open with the magic. Then Gilda might tap-dance, doing imitations of Pinky Lee or Mr. Bojangles. Bill Murray often regaled us with his amazingly wacko lounge singer act, on one occasion playing a hysterically mispronounced "Harvar Nargila" on a ukulele the size of his thumb.

Then, as the evening progressed, Belushi never failed to have us shaking with laughter at his food fight foreshadowings in the kitchen.

I don't know if the following incident was the inspiration for the famous food fight scene in *Animal House*. Belushi always enjoyed the fact that he was known by some of his friends as "America's guest" because of his habit of entering a house, going right to the refrigerator, making himself a sandwich, turning on the television, and taking his snack to the host's couch or favorite armchair and settling down as if he owned the place. It was not uncommon for him to fall asleep and stay the night. I never heard of anyone who was offended by this behavior—even total strangers, whose houses he had no qualms about entering. On the contrary, he was such an endearing, bighearted fellow that you were happy he was making himself so comfortable.

As Dan Aykroyd put it at Belushi's funeral: "He was a good man . . . but a bad boy!"

Anyway, one night John was at Gilda's house. I think Gilda's friend Dale was there, along with some hangers-on whom I did not know, probably friends of Dale's, including two really nice-looking, sexy women and a kind of dorky guy from California who was desperately trying to suck up to the stars. I don't remember his name, nor how he happened to be there. He was very fastidious and dainty, which was hard because Gilda had put out a heap of slobbery food she had bought at Zabar's. I remember an oily, garlicky salad made of asparagus spears, some mashed potatoes, some cranberry sauce, chicken wings, and the centerpiece of the spread, an enormous bowl of fruit salad. In addition to Mr. California's efforts to eat without soiling his lips, you could see that he was enormously impressed with himself because he was in the same room as Gilda and John Belushi. He was desperately trying to make a good impression.

Gilda treated him kindly, as she did everyone. But unfortunately for him, he offended Belushi immediately by trying to make a joke that was clearly stolen from a contemporary source. If you are going to borrow, at least borrow from something in a foreign language. God help you in this company if you stole a known joke and tried to present it as your own—especially if the source was trying to make an honest living. But this ill-starred fellow did exactly that, by saying, with a faked-up sigh:

"I don't want a career. I want a careen."

That mildly amusing line first appeared in a book called *Person to Person* by Barry Stevens, and it had been reprinted in the *Whole Earth Catalog.* Naturally Belushi was intimately familiar with that publication. All of America's sacred cows were his meat and milk. He had even been part of the *National Lampoon* gang that mercilessly parodied the *Catalog* in an affectionate effort to get it to renounce or at least violate what Tony Hendra has called the California Code of Uniform Consciousness.

Belushi pounced.

He picked up one of the asparagus spears, dripping with oil and spices, and lashed it lightheartedly about Mr. California's well-scrubbed face.

"We got a whole careen full of asparagus right here," Belushi said in his humorously menacing tone and flung a brace of the vegetables onto Mr. C's shoulder.

Gilda went:

"Eeek, Belush."

Mr. California was stunned and appeared to have turned to stone.

But Belushi was not to be stopped. Next came the mashed potatoes, which Belushi threw with unerring accuracy, his aim sharpened by years of snowball fighting in Chicago. A potato blob got Mr. C right in the face, and suddenly this quiet little gathering turned into a real jamboree.

To the accompaniment of loud shouts, everybody began springing up and flinging whatever they could find. Croutons, peas, muffins, bars of butter—nothing was spared. It is lucky that Gilda was not a good cook and that she did not have any splattery soufflés or other scalding entrees at hand, because Mr. California tried to give back as good as he got, upsetting the food table in the process.

For a big guy, Belushi was very quick. He managed to

save the fruit salad just as it was about to overturn onto the floor. As he picked up the bowl, he turned and found himself behind Mr. California, who was busy dousing one of the girls with cranberry sauce. In spite of the hail of produce and chicken wings, Belushi managed to immobilize the crowd as he raised the bowl high above his head and crowned Mr. California with an enormous quantity of fruit salad.

As thc Albanian Devil struck, he yelled at the top of his lungs the immortal phrase

"*Eat a bowl of fuck*!"

We all rolled on the floor with laughter, helpless. Even Mr. C eventually had to admit he had never had so much fun in his countercultural life.

The next day Gilda had to pay her housekeeper double to clean up the mess.

That Belushian phrase "Eat a bowl of fuck" became a password of the "SNL" troupe, one of the few genuinely funny things drawn from their lives that was never able to find its way onto television.

In the same way Belushi was merciless to mugwumps, he was the most generous man in the world to people he liked. In this he and Gilda were very similar.

One day at the "SNL" office Gilda said to Belushi: "How can we help out Meat Loaf?"

The portly musician was a favorite of the troupe, and they were trying to help his career, which, for some reason, had gotten stuck after his first album came out.

The next day I happened to be at Belushi's apartment on Bleecker Street. The enfant terrible of the airwaves was sweet as pie as he talked on thc phone to his agent, Bernie:

"Say, listen. Meat Loaf is a friend of mine and . . ."

It was not long afterward that Meat Loaf appeared on "Saturday Night," and his career got back on track.

As "Saturday Night" changed from a wild experiment to the hottest show on TV to a going concern, Gilda became amused by the changing modes of transportation she and the rest of the cast utilized to go to work.

In the first season they all took the subway or bus. If they were feeling flush or if, like Gilda, they had some money, they might splurge and take a taxi. When it was time to go home, after a show, at two o'clock in the morning, they would hail cabs, preferably big Checkers, to go to the party as cheaply as possible. Then, after the party, they would all hope to be lucky enough to find cabs to take them home.

The second show, in October 1975, was a music special featuring the reunion of Simon and Garfunkel. After the show there was a splendid party in a flat on Washington Square Park, in the Village. After the party broke up, Gilda could not find a cab. She was staying at a hotel because she had not yet sublet the apartment on Eighty-Fourth Street. But no cab—she had to walk. She could not get over how she went straight from appearing on national television to walking alone, like a derelict, all the way up Sixth Avenue at four o'clock in the morning.

Tim "Andre" Davis picked up Gilda twice during this period, in his New York City medallion taxicab. He became so intrigued with Gilda, fell so in love with her, that he decided to become a comedian himself. As of this writing Tim "Andre" has already appeared in a segment of "48 Hours" and is about to appear in a small feature film and a Viacom comedy special called "Outrageous Taxi Stories."

"I picked her up. It wasn't right at 30 Rock, but she was walking on Sixth Avenue. It was like six o'clock on a Monday evening, in the summer. Must have been '75 or '76. Right away, we began to talk. Now, I picked up a lotta stars, and let me tell you. Most of them are a pain in the ass. But not Gilda. She was lovely, just lovely from the first minute she got in.

"As soon as I start to drive, she says she's just gotta have some McDonald's french fries. She says no one makes 'em like McDonald's. I think it's 'cause they're presalted or something. Anyway, I tell her there's a McDonald's over on Eighth Avenue and Fifty-Fourth Street, so she says, 'Fine, step on it.' "

Stopping off for food in a taxi was very characteristic of Gilda. Eric Pergeaux and I both had the experience of riding uptown with her from the Village to NBC and stopping as many as five times, once to get a bag of cookies, once for ice cream, once for doughnuts, and so on.

"We go to the McDonald's," Tim "Andre" continued, "and as we pull up, she says to me:

" 'Listen, you know, I'm a big star already, and if I go in there they're gonna mob me. Will you come in there with me?' "

"Now, I'm a big man."

Tim "Andre" paused at this point, so, in case you haven't already noticed, you can take in the fact that he is six feet six inches tall and weighs nearly three hundred pounds.

"So I go in there with her, kinda like pretending I'm her bodyguard. I mean I really *was* her bodyguard, you know what I mean? And the place is full of people staring at her, but because I'm so big they don't dare come close.

"So we go in, and just like a normal person she walks right up to the counter and orders two orders of french fries. The normal size.

"She pays and gives me one of the orders of fries. So we walk out eating them. And they really are good.

"We get back in the cab, and we eat our fries together

and laugh as I'm driving her down to the Village. She tells me how glad she is for once to be able just to walk into a restaurant like a normal human being.

"I felt so privileged to have played a role with Gilda Ratner."

Here, unfortunately, Tim "Andre" made the slip that Gilda hated, mangling her name. But she would certainly have forgiven him in this case, because of the fries.

A few months later I was riding in a taxi up Hudson Street when I spotted Belushi hitchhiking uptown with a vengeance. He could not get a cab to save his life, and he was jumping up and down in frustration and yelling "Fuck you!" at the top of his lungs, one of his favorite pastimes.

I asked my driver to stop, and we went backward about two hundred yards to pick up Belushi.

He watched warily as we approached in reverse. When he saw it was me, he broke into a smile and clambered quickly into the cab.

"Where to, Belush?" I asked.

"Thank God." He sighed anxiously. He was beside himself with nervousness. "I gotta be at Radio City like forty-five minutes ago, and they'll have my ass on toast for sure."

"Radio City and step on it!" I ordered the driver. I said to Belushi:

"I've always wanted to tell a taxi driver to step on it!"

He laughed.

The driver did as he was bidden, and in record time we pulled up to the Fiftieth Street entrance of NBC.

"Thanks a lot," Belushi said. "I really owe you."

"Don't mention it," I said and waved him on.

A couple of days later I ran into Belushi on Bleecker Street.

"Did they roast your ass the other day at NBC?" I inquired.

"Aww, shit, man," he replied sheepishly. "It was the wrong day!"

The second season of "Saturday Night," NBC shook the old sock and allowed cast members and other late-night workers to call and order taxis to take them home after hours. This is a standard network perk for shows that are making money. Gilda, Jane, and Belushi would share one cab going to the Village. Laraine and some of the others would share another going to the Upper West Side, where Laraine had rented Gilda's old blue flat on Eighty-Fourth and Riverside.

By the third year, after Gilda had already won an Emmy, each star got his or her own personal taxi account. Every Saturday night, seven taxis were lined up outside 30 Rockefeller Plaza.

By the next year that had changed to seven limousines. Gilda used to laugh about the nights she, Belushi, and Jane Curtin were all riding down Fifth Avenue in their personal limos, three abreast, waving to one another and talking on their car telephones.

Gilda, Kitty, and Ellen were at the show one Saturday night and preparing to ride downtown to the party. They got into one of the limos in front of NBC. But the driver refused to take them because it was Belushi's limo, not Gilda's. Hers had apparently had some trouble and was going to be late. But the driver had his orders and refused to give them a ride without Belushi. Since only God knew when Belushi would deign to visit the party, the old friends all laughed and hailed a taxi.

On the way downtown, Ellen asked Gilda about Lily Tomlin, who had been the guest host that night.

"What's she like?" Ellen asked.

"Well, she may seem nice," Gilda said. "But she's always trying to one-up everybody and upstage everybody on the show."

"Really?" Ellen said in disbelief.

"Yes. And you know what? They all do. Every one of those guest hosts is so ambitious and so insecure they can't stand it if you take the attention away from them."

"Haven't you even had one you liked?" Kitty asked.

"You know who was my favorite?" Gilda said. "Ralph Nader."

"Come with me, Dave. I'll introduce you to all the right people," Gilda said. Over the next few years she kept her promise.

Once she introduced me to Tom Schiller, an "SNL" writer, at the Sevilla restaurant. It was my birthday, and Gilda had arranged a little dinner party.

"You guys should really get to know each other," she says as Schiller and I shake hands. "Tom is an Aries too."

"Top of the zodiac to ya," I say, and all laugh.

I sat down to a delightful dinner, on Gilda. There were six of us, and we ate shrimp diablo and shrimp with wine sauce and drank pitcher after pitcher of Sevilla's excellent red sangria. Gilda helped finish everyone's dessert.

Schiller had a strong interest in spiritual exercises, and he wanted to talk about t'ai chi. Gilda had told him I practiced it, and he was interested, although he masked his interest with a challenge.

"I heard that if you do t'ai chi your whole body changes," he said with a skeptical undertone in his voice. "I don't think I want my whole body to change."

"You're not in *that* great shape," I replied offhandedly. "Besides, it still stays *your* body. Two eyes, a nose, and a mouth. It just works better."

"Dave does it every day," Gilda said. She had always been impressed by my body's dedication to itself.

Schiller and I liked each other, but I always felt he was wary of the t'ai chi. The last thing any Saturday Nighter could afford to do was to fall under the spell of fanatics. They were here to attack fanaticism, not participate in it.

Schiller was one of the few who appreciated Gilda's dramatic abilities at "Saturday Night." It was he who produced the classic *La Dolce Gilda*. As Schiller characterized her in that film, all her life Gilda was a team player. She functioned best in an ensemble. In high school it was with her girlfriends. In college it was with me and our Michigan Mafia. In show biz it was with her coplayers. In life it was usually with her circle of friends.

Nevertheless, as Schiller also picked up, from time to time she went into semiseclusion. It never lasted long. She referred to it once as "one time when I was being a bag lady. . . ."

She always felt a special kinship with bag ladies, derelicts, and the unfortunate. We would sometimes walk down the street, and she would see some homeless hobo and say, very quietly:

"I could be that person."

In moods like this she would often go out in disguise, visit the open-air markets on Orchard Street or in SoHo, and fill her shopping bags with little pieces of junk. Perhaps she wanted to see how it felt to be one of them; she certainly looked like a bag lady. She also used the disguise as a duck blind, so she could stare at people without having them stare back at her. Her fame did not allow her to be a normal observer anymore.

"For comedy you've got to be an audience," she said. "If you don't wait for your laughs, you don't get them. So you have to be watching yourself at the same time. And in order to develop material, you can't always be onstage. You've got to be watching, too. If I can't go to a grocery store and do my shopping and say to myself, 'Look at that lady over there, that's really weird,' because she's looking at me, then I've lost my school."

Once she had restored her inner balance and had enough of "school," she would shed her disguise and reemerge with new wings, ready once again to fly with the squadron.

Ever wringing humor out of pain, Gilda took some of her funniest stories from her dentist's office.

Gilda's teeth and gums always gave her a hard time. She regularly visited her dentist, Dr. Paul Scheier, whose office is on the ground floor of a building on Central Park South, just off Columbus Circle, within walking distance of Radio City.

Once, in her early days in New York, Dr. Scheier had temporarily removed her many caps, revealing shaved-down stumps of teeth. Before he could put in the replacement caps, Gilda suddenly tore herself out of the chair and, in a lightning-quick movement, shoved two of those absorbent cotton cylinders into her mouth, like two fangs.

She then ran outside, still in her drool bib, onto Central Park South. To the startled looks of passersby, she flashed her tooth stumps and the two cotton fangs and broke into an insane, maniacal laugh.

She then banged on Dr. Scheier's ground-floor window with all her might, crying, in a demented, drooling voice:

"Give me my teeth! Give me my teeth!"

On another occasion Dr. Scheier sent her to an oral surgeon, fearing she might need to have her gums scraped for gingivitis. Before the final scraping could be done, a tooth had broken, root canal and all, leaving a sort of L-shaped shell. A specialist was indicated.

With her heart in her boots, Gilda gamely visited the specialist, Dr. Sherwood I believe his name was. He filled her mouth with various metal clamps and rubber plugs and examined away.

It was Gilda's curse this time to be "dentally interesting." Her teeth sent Dr. Sherwood into flights of dental ecstasy.

"Hmm. Wow. Yeah," he muttered, as his hands worked busily around her bicuspids. Then he abruptly pulled out of her mouth and, without even taking off his rubber gloves, got on the telephone.

"Hey, Bill, listen to this. I got a girl here, and she's got an L-transverse on the second bicuspid. . . ."

He then calls up two more dentists and has conversations that strike the fear of God into Gilda.

"What do you think, Joe? Can I scrape it without an E-X? Oh, really? It would? Wow, glad I talked to you. . . ."

"Hey, Bob, did you ever hear of an L-transverse on the second bicuspid? Do you think I need to extract the flange before scraping? . . . No kidding!"

Suddenly, as if this weren't bad enough, a perfect stranger suddenly appears in the examining room and puts his hands into Gilda's mouth!

"Who are you?" she exclaims, as loudly and as best she can with a mouthful of metal and cotton.

"Oh," says Dr. Sherwood, "I forgot to introduce you. This is *my* dentist!"

It was after one of Gilda's root canal sessions that she demonstrated to my friend Vic her true largeness of heart. Vic was always a great storyteller, so here's the story in his own words:

"This was in the winter of 1978. There was a lot of snow

on the ground, I remember. I was in New York repping some Pan Am flight attendants."

Vic is now a lawyer, but in those days he was a union organizer. He was particularly fond of his association with Pan Am's flight attendants, since it gave him many chances to do big favors for beautiful women.

"I called you, Dave, from the Hotel Kitano on Park Avenue, and right away you said, 'Vic, great to hear your voice. Get some women and come over here. You're just a five-minute taxi ride away.' "

I don't recall these exact words, but it could have happened.

"And then I asked you,'Dave, you know I'm a big fan of Gilda's. I'd give anything to meet her. Do you think you can set it up? It'll be me and my friend Shosten, one of the flight attendants.'

"You said, 'I don't know, but she just lives around the corner from me, so if she's home we might be able to make it happen. Let me give her a call.' "

In general I never honored such requests from people. But Vic was another one of my closest friends, and he is such a charming fellow that I was sure Gilda would like him. So I gave her a call.

As it turned out, she had just had a root canal that very morning, and of course she was feeling terrible. I immediately begged off, saying "Forget it, we'll do it another time." But I was amazed when she insisted that I bring them over, saying maybe it would help her forget the pain in her teeth. So I called Vic back.

" 'She's home,' you told me. 'But she's just had a root canal, and she wants to rest for an hour.' So she suggested, 'Why don't you guys have dinner first and then come over for dessert?'

"So we all had dinner someplace in the Village. I remember, you paid and you were very proud to be able to pay. You were finally starting to make some money, I guess.

"After dinner, we all went over to Gilda's. We went in, the door opened, and there she was, walking down this huge stairway like she was making an entrance in some Hollywood film of the thirties. But her mouth was all like this." He blew out his cheek, imitating someone who's just had a root canal.

The way I recall this, Vic and Shosten were looking at Gilda with *their* mouths wide open. They could not believe they were really in the presence—in the home!—of this huge international star. Gilda picked right up on this, in spite of her discomfort. I vividly remember Gilda's first words to them:

"Come on in, make yourselves at home, don't worry about anything."

"So we went in," Vic continues, "and she was, she was—totally Gilda! It wasn't another person that you saw on TV. She looked just the same, like her, and she was funny like her.

"We all had dessert, and then we went into this little room to the right of her living room and—I don't know if you want to print this part—we smoked a joint.

"I thought to myself, Oh, God, I'm smoking a joint with Gilda.

"I thought I was being so witty and funny that night that I said to myself, My God, I'm so funny I'm giving her material!"

The way I remember it, Vic and Shosten sat quiet as mice, watching TV. I don't remember any smoking. But Gilda liked them and repeatedly said:

"Don't worry about anything."

She seemed concerned that she might make them feel strange, and she was doing her best to make them comfortable in her presence. They were.

"It was like we had known her all our lives," Shosten

recalls, echoing Vic. "She was so funny and cute and all puffed up from the root canal. We loved her."

Vic continues: "We stayed there for a long time. As we were getting ready to leave, bundling up, I said to her:

" 'Gilda, can I ask you something?'

" 'Sure,' she said.

" 'Can I kiss you?'

"She laughed and stuck her cheek out.

" 'No,' I said, 'I mean on the lips, a real kiss?'

"She laughed and said, 'Well, that's fine!'

"So I kissed her on the lips, and we left."

Because of her teeth and some mysterious problem with her saliva, Gilda was always a gum junkie.

She was constantly chewing, at least a pack of sugarless a day, with a stick or two of sugared thrown in. She particularly liked bubble gum, and her wrecking-ball purse and her apartment always used to smell of that curious kind of finely powdered sugar and saccharin they put in bubble gum, mixed with the scent of cigarettes.

For she also loved to smoke, until she found out she was sick. But until then she was never without a couple of cartons of Benson & Hedges Longs. One of her characteristic nontheatrical poses was sitting at a café table, right elbow on the table, right fist loosely held against her cocked head, left elbow also on the table, with her left hand holding the burning cigarette up at a forty-five-degree angle, thumb on the cool tip.

In this posture she would invariably be staring, listening intently.

It was not until the second year of "Saturday Night Live" that Gilda deliberately became bulimic, before most people had ever heard of that word. She taught herself to throw up. She tried to keep it secret, but once she even blurted to a reporter that she had thrown up in every bathroom in Rockefeller Center.

She confided to me that it was a result of her fame and the constant display of her image on television.

"Dave," she'd say as she stuffed one of Kitty's fish sandwiches into her mouth, "I'm almost afraid to eat. I want desperately to be as thin as Laraine. But food is my only comfort in life."

Another time she said: "I'm a compulsive eater and also a compulsive dieter. That's the only way to stay thin."

Gilda was a walking, fressing encyclopedia when it came to restaurants in Greenwich Village. She knew every one of them intimately. She knew their hours of operation, their specialties, and every detail about them except one—their prices. She did not care about price in the least. All she wanted was a place she could find doughnuts at three o'clock in the morning.

She loved to make up new names for restaurants, especially when they displeased her: Under the Trees was a place she avoided and called "Under the Trees Where Nobody Goes." She had tried a certain Bleecker Street soul-food place a few times. It had a great-sounding menu, but little bits of detritus always seemed to find their way into her food. Finally she made up a new menu, suspiciously reminiscent of some of the things she thought she had eaten in Paris. The principal item was the delectable "Toenail Soup."

Her pattern of purging began to overwhelm her life. She never failed to be totally professional about her work. But her private life became a blitz of bingeing, then a purgatory of prophylaxis. I felt it was an echo of her old fat days. Food and love were always the two areas of her life that were out of control. Using comedy, she could control her environment. Using money, she could control her circumstances. But when she came under pressure, the part of her that broke was what went into and came out of her mouth.

Bulimia ended when she fell in love with Gene. But unfortunately, her eating habits changed violently after she was sick, after she was forced to fast for a long time. When she finally began to eat again, she abandoned her erstwhile ways and put herself on a one-menu diet: white meat of chicken with mustard and green beans. She ate the same meal every day. She gave up alcohol for good, and she also gave up her beloved tuna fish.

Gilda's bingeing period, approximately from 1977 to 1979, was a time of great inner turmoil and intense creative activity. During this era she occasionally took on a job outside of "Saturday Night." She played Jill of Hearts in the television rock musical "Jack: A Flash Fantasy" on PBS in 1977. She did the voice of the title character in an animated Halloween special called "Witch's Night Out" on NBC in 1979. And she appeared in a segment of the movie *Mister Mike's Mondo Video* in 1979, an hour-long mock documentary written and produced by Michael O'Donoghue. It was full of sketches rejected by NBC as violations of good taste and "standards and practices." It picked up a cult following, but movie critics generally panned it as "sick" and "obscenely pointless." As Mister Mike himself has pointed out, those are just old fartly euphemisms for "funny."

One night in July 1977, Gilda called me from the Red Lion Inn in Stockbridge, Massachusetts. She had never lost her preference for the theater, and on hiatus from "Saturday Night," she was up there doing summer stock at the Berkshire Theatre Festival.

She had the role of Billie Moore, the "sweet ingenuous good girl of backstage dreams" in the old George Abbott hit *Broadway*. She loved this play because it gave her a chance to do something she had wanted to do her whole life long: to tap-dance on stage.

She had called to tell me she had met one of the girls of my ever-expanding "past" and was dancing with her eight times a week. It was none other than the charming and delightfully malicious Jeanne DeBaer, one of my first high school girlfriends.

I was not at all sure what Jeanne and Gilda were discussing on my account. Gilda's knowing laugh over the wire fed my worst fears.

After two years of "Saturday Night," Gilda thoroughly enjoyed doing theater once again. She was excellent in her role, although, as Mel Gussow observed in his *New York Times* review, she was "miscast as the ingenue. The role is one-tone, offering this marvelous comedienne no opportunity to use her primary assets—her malleable voice, quizzical double-takes and look of eternal bedazzlement. On 'Saturday Night Live,' Miss Radner is a woman possessed by clownish spirits. . . ."

But Gilda was not doing the show to clown. She had had enough clowning for a while. Gilda wanted to dance!

"Do you tap-dance?" Dennis Grimaldi, the choreographer, had asked her at the audition for *Broadway.* Like the true blue ingenue of Broadway she was to play, she lied her head off:

"Are you kidding? Of course!"

"When I found out she couldn't dance a step, that became our little secret," Dennis says with a laugh. "She didn't have to tap all that well for the show," Dennis says, "so I taught her the basics in two weeks' rehearsal at Stockbridge.

"She enjoyed it so much she continued studying with me three times a week back in New York," Dennis said at a rehearsal studio that is now the site of the Symphony Café near Carnegie Hall.

"And Gilda soon became an excellent tap dancer. She wanted to know the intricacies of every step. How does this muscle work? How is that supposed to feel?

" 'Your left foot is the drum,' I would tell her. 'Your right is the flute.'

"She would ask me things like 'How would Gene Kelly do this one? What about Cyd Charisse?—Love those long legs! What about Ellen?—Love that ponytail!' "

Gilda was in her element.

Even if clownish spirits did not get to appear onstage in Stockbridge, they did come out during the "high teas" Gilda arranged at the Red Lion Inn. She invited all the women in the show, and it was a dressy affair: all were required to wear rubber hats and rubber gloves.

Soon, all the men in the show began to crash the weekly tea, also wearing assorted rubber goods of varying sizes.

That provoked a series of outdoor barbecues for the rest of the summer, at which the main attraction quickly shifted from rubber to food—mainly betting on how much food Gilda was going to eat.

"It was absolutely phenomenal how much she could eat," Jeanne DeBaer commented. "At one I remember she ate three cheeseburgers, two hot dogs, then pigged out on s'mores! We couldn't figure out where she put it all!" Then she added, on a somber note, "Now, of course, we know."

In fact, although she tried to keep it secret, some did know of her eating problem even then. Victor Garber enrolled Gilda in a local bulimia clinic in the Berkshires. She went for a couple of weeks and seemed to improve. But then she relapsed into her old habit of eating to come down.

Jeanne had fallen in love with Gilda directly upon the issuance of costumes for the girls in the chorus. They were the revealing tights known as "scanties," typical of chorines of the Roaring Twenties. Immediately after they were passed out, Gilda distributed plastic razors attached to signs that read:

"I ain't shavin' my pussy for no summer stock!"

In that department Gilda, at the time, was "having a bit of a fling" with Chris Sarandon, the male lead in *Broadway*, who was playing the oh-so-seductive criminal cad Steve Crandall.

After the show was over, Chris invited her down to see him, at a house in Brazil. It would be Gilda's first trip abroad, not counting Canada, since her horrific days in Europe more than ten years before. She was terribly excited to go, owing to Chris's soon-to-be-availability after a messy divorce from his wife, Susan. Chris had done very well in real estate and, among other properties, had come into temporary possession of François De Menil's house on Búzios, a chic island near Rio de Janeiro.

In those days Gilda detested foreign travel, having had the bad dose of it described earlier. But with Gilda love conquered all—she accepted.

Shortly afterward, Gilda called my Brazilian fiancée on the phone, crying like a baby.

"Do you need any Brazilian money?" Gilda asked through her tears. "I've got a whole bunch of it right here, and I can't stand looking at it; it makes me so depressed. . . ."

"Were you in Brazil?" my girlfriend asked, surprised she had heard nothing of this trip before.

"I was there for a total of eight hours." Gilda laughed and sniffled. "I spent more time in the plane than in all of Brazil."

Isa invited her over, and in our living room on Perry Street, around the corner from her house, she recounted the story of Chris's invitation and its acceptance:

"When I got to his house, there were all these naked broads lounging around the swimming pool. I was shocked. And then Chris came over, with a couple of them draped around him, like this."

Demonstrating like a sexy Olive Oyl rag doll, she gave the words her particular emphasis, something like Roseanne Roseannadanna would have done, only softer, with a touch of pathos.

"I kind of gestured to Chris, like could he come over here and talk for a minute. But he refused! He wouldn't uncoil from those . . . those . . . bombshells! I couldn't believe my eyes. So I turned them away. I began to stare at the wallpaper, thinking, What should I do? Suddenly, I realized the wallpaper was full of these little clever prints of people *fucking* in all these different positions! I couldn't stand it, so I turned right around and went home! I told you, I spent less time in Brazil than in the plane!"

We laughed, remembering her first trip to Europe.

"You're allergic to foreign countries," I said.

"Except Canada," agreed Gilda. "You don't have to fly to get to Canada."

On the return trip, she went on, she had met Mike Nichols in the plane. Because of bad weather in New York, they circled and circled, and Gilda, not a good traveler in any case, got nervous. As usual, she let it out in joke form.

"I can't believe you're on this plane, Mike," she said to him. "If I'd been here without you and we crashed, the headline would read, 'Gilda Killed in Air Crash.' Now that you're here, the headline will read, 'Mike Nichols Killed in Crash,' and then, at the end of the story, on page seventy-three, it will say, in small print, 'Also dead, G. Radner.' "

The show, *Broadway*, was so good it went onto Broadway itself in the fall.

"Gilda was crushed that she had to drop out of it because of 'Saturday Night Live,' " recalls Dennis Grimaldi. "More than anything in the world, she wanted to tap-dance on Broadway. She told me her father would have been so proud of her. . . . But frankly, I think she really wanted to show up her mother."

Glenn Close eventually got her role on Broadway and, according to the buzz, got Chris Sarandon as well.

"She became family," said Dennis Grimaldi with a fond smile of recollection. It was the kind of epithet nearly everyone used about her. It was not always the same phrase, but always something like that.

Like Dennis, everyone who got to know Gilda well soon felt her become part of their family. And, of course, she "knew" millions of people. As she put it once in a magazine article:

"Maybe you know me or maybe you don't or maybe you heard of me but never saw me or maybe you used to know me but don't know me anymore, but whatever or wherever I am today and whether you know me or not, for one time in my life and yours I was famous and it seemed like everyone knew me."

She herself felt that her family life had been cruelly cut off. Unconsciously or half-consciously she tried to make the whole world her family. She is truly remarkable in that she succeeded.

"She loved me because I could cook," Dennis says with a laugh.

During the autumn after Stockbridge, Dennis Grimaldi's cooking ability led to a series of exceedingly pleasant and euphoric tap-dancing Saturday lunches at 92 Charles Street. Gilda loved this apartment because the living room had a small elegant stage built in. I don't know its original use, but she frequently used it as a tap-dancing platform. These lunches became tap-a-cooking extravaganzas. Dennis would tap into the dining room with some lovely concoction he had whipped up.

One of Gilda's favorites she called "Dennis's Lobster Oscar." It was made from veal cutlets simmered in wine, then covered with sautéed fresh lobster meat. Each portion was topped with asparagus tips and drizzled with *sauce béarnaise.*

Tap-dancing all the way, Gilda would take this delicious concoction on a platter and dance around to the other guests, offering each a cutlet accompanied by some château potatoes. Then she would tap her way back into the kitchen and eat more herself before exchanging the platter for another.

These lunches often extended into dinners, and it was not uncommon for everyone to fall asleep in her purple plush furniture and get up together for breakfast on Sunday morning.

Gilda did not return to New York empty-handed, or, shall we say, empty-footed. After her summer in Stockbridge she strode into Lorne Michaels's office back on the seventeenth floor of Rockefeller Center. Breaking into a rocking, socking tap dance, she cried, "Hey, Lorne—look what I can do!"

Her tap dancing convinced Lorne to give Dennis a job as choreographer on "Saturday Night Live," and together Dennis and Gilda created the dancing N that occasionally graced the airwaves.

By this time in the history of "SNL," Lorne was lord and master of all he surveyed.

A Canadian Jew, he had emerged from the Land of Clean Beaver and without warning established around himself the most illustrious salon in the world. Tony Hendra dubbed him the "El Cid of Satire."

Like "a one-man Muslim horde," Lorne took over NBC's famous Studio 8-H after having haunted the halls of American humor, especially The Committee (a San Francisco offshoot of Second City), for many years.

According to Hendra's excellent history of modern American comedy, *Going Too Far*, "two things brought life to *Saturday Night* for Michaels. The first was the fact that NBC—trailing badly in the ratings—was anxious to launch a series aimed at the eighteen-to-thirty-fours. The second was that Michaels discovered New York and *The National Lampoon*."

That, of course, included Gilda, the key instrument in Lorne's plan to "discover New York."

When Gilda and I were in college, we used to delight in reading, out loud, old Robert Benchley stories and Fred Allen sketches. Little did we imagine that not so far in the future she would inherit Fred Allen's mantle, hanging on a hook in the same legendary Studio 8-H at NBC. Boy, did it need airing out!

If the walls of Studio 8-H could talk, they would repeat some very funny things indeed. Behind those double yellow doors, more than anywhere, was the history of American broadcast comedy made.

Lorne was made for Studio 8-H. A theatrically oriented executive producer, he always sits not in the control room but on the floor. But he is always watching a monitor, not the floor itself, and he is usually accompanied by a very good-looking assistant and a goblet of white wine. He is a handsome man, totally charming, most intelligent—yet you can sense the tinge of vulnerability, perhaps a hidden touch of erstwhile inferiority that he is covering up strongly. Or perhaps there is just a paranoia in there that emanates. After all, he's Jewish. But he can sure work a room and is absolute master of the studio's large floor and small gallery.

Lorne has done brilliantly with his formula. The only "criticism" of him you hear from other, less notorious comedy producers is that he is a one-trick pony.

"Ask him if he can do anything besides 'Saturday Night Live,'" one illustrious comedy producer advised me when told I was going to interview Lorne. Lorne was ready for the question and pointed to movies like *¡Three Amigos!* But I could tell the question rankled him; perhaps because it's something he suspects about himself. His attempt to create a sequel to "SNL," "The New Show," was an unmitigated disaster. The primary problem was that the show was *not* new. It was like the worst attempt to imitate his original hit, worse even than "Fridays."

Lorne now seems to have made peace with this. After several years bashing about in the Beverly Hills jungle, he has returned to the show he created and continues to do his sterling job as executive producer. He is doing what he does best.

Gilda always loved and respected Lorne and felt he could do no wrong.

"He has an amazing way of seeing talent," she said, and in this you really have to admire his taste. He chose the best: Gilda, Belushi, and the Murrays from the *Lampoon* show, O'Donoghue and Beatts from the *Lampoon* magazine, and so on through the years.

About Gilda, Lorne was equally enthusiastic: "Gilda is still very innocent and un-starlike," he said in an interview. "She never says things like, 'Is this part *right* for Gilda Radner?' Her biggest strength is a very large and good heart and it comes across on the air. That's why she was one of the first people our audience picked up on."

Lorne sometimes referred to her vulnerable childlike quality as the "Muppet factor."

Gilda was very dedicated to the writers on the show. She was a great improviser but never liked to write until after she left television. I believe it was the solitariness of staring at the paper that put her off. She needed to be with people to cook.

A prime practitioner of Gilda's style of comedy was the excellent writer Marilyn Suzanne Miller.

In addition to the aforementioned "Slumber Party" number, some of Gilda's most notable sketches are collaborations with Marilyn: "Goodbye Saccharin," the Judy Miller pieces.

Gilda's other favorite writers were Alan Zweibel and Tom Schiller. Zweibel had done his apprenticeship in the Borscht Belt, writing one-liners for Morty Gunty and other old-time comics. Lorne hired him for the one-liners, but he soon became the man behind Emily Litella and Roseanne Roseannadanna.

Zweibel is a man-mountain, a smiling blond Jewish giant with muscles like iron bands. On June 28, 1976, during the hiatus after the first season of "Saturday Night," Zweibel, his girlfriend, Robin, and I took Gilda out for a special and memorable birthday dinner.

During this era Gilda's favorite restaurant in New York was a place on 114th Street and Pleasant Avenue, in Spanish Harlem. There was no name on the outside, but it was known to one and all in the vicinity as Rao's. Just down the street, on Pleasant, was the candy store belonging to the infamous "Un Occhio," One-Eye, who, according to *New York Newsday* columnist Jimmy Breslin, is the boss of all crime in America. When Un Occhio slammed his telephone down on the Formica counter of his candy store, his pet wolf, stretched out on the floor, would pick up his head, bare his teeth, and growl so loud you could hear him up and down the block. Even though this is officially "Harlem," this little corner of East Harlem is a model neighborhood, elegant, clean, and conspicuously crime-free. Un Occhio makes sure of that, from his candy store and from his all-marble house on a side street off First Avenue.

Originally Rao's was just a restaurant for the people in the neighborhood—in other words, for Un Occhio and his clan. For eighty years it had been so, until Gilda, in her insatiable quest for food, discovered it. She was the first outsider ever permitted to eat there, and somehow her charms soothed the savage beasts who hitherto had kept all interlopers away with deathlike stares and bared fangs. So it was there that Zweibel, Robin, and I took Gilda for her thirtieth birthday.

We walked in, in the middle of summer, and saw the inevitable Christmas decorations hung all around. Several intimately autographed pictures of Frank Sinatra hung on the walls. It is a small place, really, with room for about thirty-five people at most. The two pay telephones in the back have contributed to severe prison overcrowding, but that's another story. We just came for dinner.

Gilda, Robin, Zweibel, and I all sat at one of the wooden tables near the jukebox. No menus were proffered. After a moment a pleasant-looking elderly woman came out, smiled at us, and gave us all glasses of iced tea.

"Hi, Mom," Gilda said. By way of explanation, she said to us: "She's like our mom tonight. Whatever she says to eat, we eat."

Indeed, orders were never taken. Without surcease throughout the evening, "Mom" continually arrived at our table bearing huge platters of steaming Italian delicacies, which we all consumed with gusto. Gilda was happy as a *vongola* and kept getting up from the table to chuck more quarters into the truly outstanding jukebox, which, in addition to a feast of Italian numbers, featured all of her favorite tunes from the fifties, including the entire repertoire from the Indian River slumber party.

Zweibel was spending the summer relaxing his mind and flexing his large muscles in front of Robin's equally large eyes. This was taking place right there at the table, with all these mob leg breakers appraising us with sidelong glances, no doubt wondering just how much torque and what stance it would take to twist Zweibel's meaty arm behind his back until it cracked.

Gilda ate an enormous amount of food, as in fact did all of us. Pitchers of wine were sluiced down like water. The music got mellower and mellower. Finally, after the umpteenth course, Gilda pushed away her plate, heaved an enormous sigh, and laughed.

"I haven't been able to eat anything for three days," she said suddenly.

All of us were amazed.

"Gilda," I said, "with your appetite? My God, you must be sick!"

"No," she said with a smile. "Nobody's asked me out to eat, that's all!"

All of us laughed.

"Was that funny?" Gilda asked with her special "wry" voice, putting her tongue between her teeth. "Why was that funny?"

Robin said, "It's just the way you say things that makes them funny. Like it's not funny, and certainly not dignified, if I say 'I gotta go to the powder conservatoire.' But suppose I say, 'I gotta go to the dumper.' Will you excuse me?"

With this she got up and matched action to word as we all laughed.

Gilda's collaboration with Zweibel began about a month into the first season. She wanted to do a sketch called

"Why I Love Being a Fireman," and she asked Zweibel to help her. They went out to dinner at Downey's Steak Pub to talk things over, and it turned into one of those Gilda dinners where all pretense falls away and communication takes place from soul to soul. Both confessed their fear of the unknown maw of television and their bedazzlement from mixing with the finest minds of their generation. In the course of the evening, and in what became the pattern for many subsequent working dinners, they ordered half the items on the menu and picked at all of them. It cost Gilda a bundle on her American Express card.

Gilda and Zweibel's first big hit was Emily Litella. Emily had first appeared in a sketch written by Gilda and Tom Davis, in which Ms. Litella is a children's book writer and is promoting a book she wrote about "itsy bitsy teeny tiny weensy beensy little things." A couple of shows later Emily did her first "Weekend Update," and Gilda, needing an out to the backchat with Chevy, first came up with her priceless "Never mind!" When Zweibel heard that, he ran with it, and partly deaf Emily began to editorialize on cures for canker, endangered feces, presidential erections, and the like. Later they followed a similar pattern with Roseanne Roseannadanna: she first appeared in a Rosie Shuster sketch called "Hire the Incompetent," then she Zweibeled to stardom.

Tom Schiller, her other favorite, had also learned at the knees of some real experts: first, his father, Bob Schiller, who had been one of the writers on "I Love Lucy." Gilda's favorite comedy sketch of all time was one she first saw when she was six years old, in 1952, the one Lucy did called "Job Switching." The plot is that in their eternal war between the sexes Lucy and Ethel switch roles with Ricky and Fred. Lucy and Ethel get jobs at a candy kitchen. After bungling their first assignments, they are transferred to the wrapping department, where they have to wrap each piece of candy as it goes by on a conveyor belt. In a scene worthy of Chaplin in *Modern Times*, the infernal machine gradually goes faster and faster, and Lucy and Ethel must stuff the candies into their hats, pockets, and blouses—and of course a great number go into their mouths.

In the same vein, Gilda often told Schiller:

"Don't worry, just give me a conveyor belt and a lot of pies."

In fact Schiller went his father one better and updated the Lucy sketch with an ending that is just about impossible to beat. In the "SNL" version, also shot in black and white, Gilda has a job in a nuclear bomb factory. Nuclear bombs come out on a conveyor belt, and Gilda has to squirt them with whipped cream and place a cherry on top of each one before putting it onto a shelf. Dan Aykroyd gives her very detailed instructions, ending with the injunction that "whatever you do, don't drop them." Naturally the belt gradually begins to convey at breakneck speeds, and Gilda is soon schlepping and juggling nuclear weapons all over the stage before the final mushroom cloud signals the commercial break.

After Schiller's apprenticeship at his father's knee, young Tom became the favorite of Henry Miller and spent considerable time with the old master, living as his surrogate son at his home in Pacific Palisades. Perhaps because of his association with Miller, Schiller brought to "SNL" a classical sensibility that showed through especially in his short films, such as the soulful, amusing *La Dolce Gilda* and the humorously prophetic *Don't Look Back in Anger.*

If Schiller had listened to Henry Miller, he would not have prostituted himself for NBC.

"Don't do it, Tom, don't do it," Miller had said when Tom asked his advice about accepting a job with Lorne. "You were made for better things."

But Schiller has a mystical bent. He believes in signs and

omens, perhaps more than the advice of friends. He consulted the ancient Chinese book of divination, the *I Ching*. Six times he threw three Chinese coins, the round ones with square holes in the center, inscribed on one side. Following the rules of the ancient oracle, asking the question, "Will this offer harm my true direction and work?" he threw the hexagram called "Abundance":

> Abundance has success.
> The king attains abundance.
> Be not sad.
> Be like the sun at midday.

Schiller ignored Miller and decided to shine like the sun at midday. His rays warmed everyone in the cast and continue to do so.

The atmosphere of the show itself was a combination of the headiness of rock and roll with the sweatiness of network television. The smell of sex was always in the air. A sign hung prominently on the studio bulletin board: "All performers must wear underwear during the show!"

The night Mick Jagger was guest host it was instantly clear that the world's greatest whoremaster was not wearing anything but skin beneath his skintight leather pants.

One of the NBC censors, whose job it is to notice such things, raised his eyebrows practically through the roof of his brain. He collared one of the production assistants on the show.

"Mick isn't wearing underwear!" the censor harrumphed portentously. "Please make sure he does."

The young woman looked at the censor as if he were an alien from the planet Mongo.

"Be my guest, Mr. Clotworthy. If you want to tell Mick

Jagger to put on underwear, go right ahead." She turned on her heel and walked out. For the record, Mick did exactly as he pleased.

Although there were well-appointed offices with actual working typewriters on the seventeenth floor, the show was often "written" under a flight of stairs on the eighth floor the day before airtime.

A knot of writers, often led by Al Franken, would stand in a stairwell outside the studio, sounding as if they were rewriting Ibsen:

"Now, the foreshadowing at the beginning sets you up for the flashback later. . . ."

During "Saturday Night," Gilda usually sat around with the writers on Monday afternoons and Tuesdays improvising. By the way, Gilda never called it "Saturday Night Live" or "SNL." She usually just referred to it as "the show."

She would sleep in her office on Tuesday nights. The writers usually worked all night on Tuesdays, and Gilda wanted to be sure she would be available if they needed her.

On the other nights in the week, even when she slept at home, she always kept the phone under the covers with her in case the writers called.

On Wednesday, Thursday, and Friday, amid an orgy of set building and people yelling into telephones, Gilda, the writers, and the rest of the team would spend all day and night rehearsing and revising.

After the Saturday dress rehearsal, there occurred one of the most pleasant, least-known features of "Saturday Night." This was the tradition of a magnificent gourmet dinner for the cast before the show.

The dinners were prepared by Kitty Shannon and her husband, Eric Pergeaux. You already know that Kitty is one of the world's premier cooks. Kitty learned to cook from Eric, who had learned it growing up in the Bordeaux region of France.

Eric has run successively successful restaurants on Shelter Island, as mentioned, and most recently on the Caribbean island of Grenada. The couple is now preparing to open a gourmet country inn in the south of France. It was Gilda who urged them to go into the restaurant business in the first place.

The "Saturday Night Live" dinners were prepared in Kitty and Eric's apartment at 31 Bank Street, for transportation and delivery to the Forty-Ninth Street loading dock of Radio City at exactly five-thirty on Saturday evening. Starting Thursday afternoon, Kitty's house became an Arab marketplace of activity, with the buying of huge quantities of hard-to-find ingredients and the marinating of vast slabs of meat.

Gilda was often in attendance while Kitty prepared these dinners.

"Gilda got me the job," Kitty recalled. "There had been another chef during the first season, but she was very unreliable. She would call from London on Saturday mornings and tell them she had missed her plane."

This redoubtable cook said she always regarded feeding "Saturday Night" as bringing food to a giant kindergarten class. She had a diploma from the Cordon Bleu in London and had cooked for a number of stars as well as "various lords and ladies on the other side of the ocean." She could never resist dropping names into her recipes. Her tabouli, for instance, was not just tabouli—it was the recipe taught to this cook's mother by King Faisal when he was a prince.

Perhaps if she had dropped only names, it would not have fallen out that, as Kitty put it, "the cast claimed they began to find fingernails in their food, and that was the end of chef number one. Gilda got me the job after an 'audition' cooking roast leg of lamb with garlic for Belushi's birthday party."

That dish intrigued Lorne enough that he visited La Terrasse on Shelter Island, and there, on the terrace that Gilda, Isa, and I helped paint, he contracted Kitty to become the "Saturday Night" cook.

Kitty's "Saturday Night" feasts were served by liveried employees of the military-industrial complex in the green room next to Studio 8-H.

In contrast to the madness and delirium swirling around outside, in the studios of the hottest television show in the world, the quiet, if not relaxed, atmosphere inside this room was always profoundly and reverently trencherlike. Even though the cast members were wired, or possibly even neurologically enhanced with doses of artificial creativity, we are talking about some major eaters, folks. Gilda and Belushi alone could put a strain on Kitty's kitchen. In every case, though, the food was more than plentiful and much too delicious to fight with or around.

"They were very fussy, very particular," Kitty recalled. "They wanted a really nice, gourmet meal, even though sometimes they were too excited to eat a lot. It didn't matter—whether they ate it or not, the hot food had to be really, really hot, and the cold stuff had to be really, really cold. It all had to look just perfect. Since there weren't any kitchen facilities there at the studio, it was really, really hard.

"One of their favorite recipes was fillet of sole in white wine sauce. I was cooking everything at my house in the Village, so I had to roll each fillet up individually and pour the white wine on. Then I had to steam it for exactly two minutes, and as quickly as I could, with three people helping me, wrap each one in foil. Then I would cook each one a little more, in the foil, so it would stay hot during the trip uptown.

"They also loved chicken in wine sauce, which we always made the French way, in a casserole with a slice of ham, two cups of warmed cognac for flame-broiling, and a cup of dry red Chambertin added immediately after the flame died down."

During the coldest part of the year the troupe often went for beef bourguignon, which Kitty made the old Provençale way. She used at least six pounds of meat for a dozen people.

Done the old French way, this is an immensely complex dish involving several stages of cutting, browning, and blending. It is fit for kings and queens of comedy.

You must cut the beef into large cubes, brown them, then sprinkle with salt, pepper, and perhaps a pinch of powdered sassafras root. A quarter cup of warmed cognac is poured over the meat and lit. When the flame dies, the beef is transferred to a casserole.

Salt pork, garlic, carrots, leeks, shallots, chopped onions, basil, chervil, tarragon, and two tablespoons of chopped fresh parsley go into a skillet and are cooked until the salt pork is crisp and the vegetables are lightly browned. The contents of the skillet go into the casserole with the beef, along with bay leaf, thyme, a little water, and a whole bottle of red Burgundy wine. It bakes for an hour and forty-five minutes.

While baking, you must make a *beurre manié* by blending one tablespoon each of butter and flour and stirring it into the casserole bit by bit. The casserole goes back into the oven for another three hours.

While that is cooking, forty small onions are browned in some butter mixed with a dash of sugar. Forty mushroom caps are sautéed in butter and olive oil until they are lightly browned on one side. Half a lemon is squeezed over them, then they are turned and browned on the other side.

When the casserole was done cooking, Kitty added the onions and put the mushrooms and parsley aside as a garnish, to be added in the green room after her mad dash to the studio.

"I needed two guys to help with the casserole and another two to take the plastic silverware—it was ridiculous to eat this great food with plastic forks and knives, but there was no place at NBC to wash dishes. We had our car then, and it was waiting outside the apartment, engine running, with Eric at the wheel. I tell you, the movie business lost a great stunt driver when Eric decided to become a chef. We made it uptown in six minutes flat.

"We needed a special pass to get into the underground parking lot at Radio City. We'd schlepp the casserole to the postal delivery dock underneath Rockefeller Center, where we'd be met by three guys with a food cart. We also had to bring tons of soda, packed in ice, and it had to be really cold. It was like feeding a small army.

"They always wanted a huge salad, full of radishes, carrots, and mushrooms, usually with my French vinaigrette dressing. That alone took two guys to carry, but at least we didn't have to worry about the temperature.

"And their favorite dessert—they could never get enough of it—cheesecake cookies. I used the recipe from the *Tassajara Bread Book*. They loved them."

Kitty's dinner hour was an important cooling-out period for the cast and writers, who were about to undergo a seven-hour blitzkrieg. Many cheesecake cookies, linzertortes, or other delectable desserts were consumed tanking up for the show.

After the meal, "Weekend Update" was rehearsed for the first time. And the cast had to learn their last-minute lines.

Gilda kept track of her changes with a yellow felt highlighter that she used to mark her script.

Dress rehearsal usually began at about eight-thirty and sometimes lasted until a quarter after eleven, leaving only fifteen minutes until the real thing. Gilda and the other cast members had a hard time learning how to hold something in reserve during dress so that they'd be able to operate at full power during the show.

Show time was always the high of the week. The audience felt special, the musicians were always hot, and the cast, writers, and crew were up for ninety minutes of the wildest live television anywhere. The control room was relatively calm for live network television. These were the best, most experienced comedy directors, cameramen, artists, and technicians in the business. Lorne sat with his goblet of white wine at a floor station just behind the set, to the left of center stage, staring into a monitor. Ernie Kovacs regularly turned over in his grave to watch.

The glamorous parties after the "Saturday Night" shows were often funnier than the shows themselves.

The social event of the 1976 season followed one of the most famous of all "Saturday Night" shows, the "Nessen show." Ron Nessen, President Ford's press secretary, was the guest host.

Nessen had agreed to guest-host the show even though Gerald Ford had been the prime object of ridicule on "Saturday Night" that year.

According to Hill and Weingrad, Nessen had happened across "SNL" one night as Chevy Chase was imitating the president. In the sketch, Nessen, played by Buck Henry, was outlining to Ford a new strategy designed to counteract the president's growing reputation for clumsiness. The notion was, "Nessen" explained, that every time Ford stumbled, so would all the aides around him, so Ford's gaffes would appear to be normal, everyday mishaps that might occur to anyone.

As Hill and Weingrad describe it, "by the end of the sketch, Chevy, Henry and two secret service agents . . . were wandering around the stage like drunken blind men, ripping their clothes, banging themselves on the head and falling on the floor."

In other sketches, Chevy, playing Ford, would take unbelievable, death-defying pratfalls. With the extra dose of energy and uncertainty that comes with live television, the audience was never sure if Chevy had not really gone too far this time and broken his back for sure. But he never once failed to open his eyes, smile to the camera, and shout: "Live, from New York! It's 'Saturday Night'!"

Nessen agreed to host the show only after inviting Chevy Chase, Dan Aykroyd, and John Belushi to the White House, where they met the president and had dinner with him at the annual banquet of the Radio and Television Correspondents Association. According to Hill and Weingrad, Chevy claims Ford splashed soup on his tux during the meal, and it took all Chevy's self-control to keep from falling off his chair with laughter.

In any case, Nessen and Ford were so impressed with the troupe they decided to let Nessen go ahead and cohost, believing this would go a long way to proving that this White House had a sense of humor even though it had pardoned Richard Nixon. Yes, Nessen really thought he was going to show the country what a cool guy Gerald Ford was. But he did not reckon with Chevy Chase's pratfalls and the spear-hand-to-the-throat poetry of the most twisted minds of our generation. The cast and writers voted with their pencils, coming up with the rankest jokes and sketches of all time.

Gilda and Zweibel's *spécialité de la maison* that night was her mock commercial for Autumn Fizz, the carbonated douche, "the douche with the effervescence of uncola." It came in various flavors, including egg cream. At the end of the commercial Gilda's tag line was "Don't leave him holding the bag." Then she burped.

A slew of NBC and Washington brass was in the audience that night, as was a counterslew of cast friends and family, including yours truly. After the show NBC threw a huge party at the Rockefeller Center skating rink. Nessen was in his cups, and he was thrilled to be seen dancing with Louise Lasser, Bette Midler, and the like (if the like exists).

Suddenly, in the middle of this party, the entire "SNL" cast and crew lit up joints simultaneously. The smell of strong, aromatic Michoacán "laughing grass" wafted gently through midtown Manhattan, and the president's main man stood smack in the middle of it with a gigantic shit-eating grin.

At the skating rink Nessen could not get enough of himself. As the boisterous evening raged on, after having had even more to drink the president's chief spokesman began to brag to the writers that he had managed to "co-opt" "Saturday Night."

Later in the morning, however, as the successive parties became more and more rarefied and the wit began to draw blood, Nessen began to realize that co-optation can be a two-way street.

Over the next few days his huge smile turned its corners downward. The consensus of the audience and the critics, who had not had nearly so much to drink as Nessen, was that "Saturday Night" had sandbagged the president on national television.

The White House, in particular, was pissed off. "Vulgar,"

"tasteless," "stupid," and "kinky" were not adjectives administration officials were accustomed to seeing in newspaper columns about the president of the United States.

Nessen gradually realized that what he and the president had perceived as the cast's helping hand of friendship was in reality the old sleeve across the windpipe. That gentle pat on the head had really been a sockful of wet sand.

As Nessen finally wrote in his memoirs, "Looking back, it's obvious that my attempt to smother the ridicule of Ford by joining the laughter on 'Saturday Night' was a failure."

As for the cast, including Gilda, they were thrilled they had finally pulled off a genuinely political act. They took full credit for the fact that Ford lost the 1976 election to Jimmy Carter.

At the height of the "Saturday Night" druggie stage, a healthy non-drug user, football star Fran Tarkenton, hosted the show. He did a parody of a public service announcement in which he pleaded for help for John Belushi, "a promising young actor whose mind was destroyed by drugs."

Belushi sat next to him in a Cub Scout uniform, staring into space.

After the show that night there was a huge party at Dan Aykroyd's loft on Bond Street in SoHo. Rock music blared from giant speakers. The most beautiful women in the world were there. There were buckets of bad medicine, with dippers. Fran Tarkenton nursed a beer all night.

Gilda, in those days, would take an occasional puff of weed. But it made her too high to function the way she wanted to.

"It gives me the whirlies," she said about marijuana that night. At this party, Gilda was the soul of conservatism, refusing all offers of weird substances and confining herself to saccharin, the one drug she truly loved and that helped make her famous.

Belushi, as ever, was another story—perhaps two other stories. He swaggered in at three o'clock in the morning, trailed by a glamorous entourage fresh from one of the various Belushi Bars he had stashed around town.

The Belushi Bar was an example of guerrilla stardom. Belushi and his entourage, numbering never fewer than ten beautiful girls, often including a judge's daughter, would blow into a rock and roll or blues bar like Trax on Seventy-Second Street and take the joint over. To this day no one knows who paid for the bottomless quantities of drink and bottomful qualities of women. Belushi invariably, around three o'clock in the morning, would commandeer the bandstand to sing a song of his own creation. One of his favorites had the title "Fuck You!" Those were also its only words, sung at the top of his oversized lungs to a heavy backbeat, in the best Blues Brother style. It never failed to bring down the house.

8

Why Gilda Left "Saturday Night"

"Those guys whose eyes look like two television sets"

"I WAS GILDA'S DATE FOR THE PREMIERE OF THE BLUES BROTHers," Miss Pat O'Donoghue remembered with a laugh. She was another old mutual friend from Ann Arbor who had also blended quickly into the mid-seventies New York high life.

"The concert took place at Carnegie Hall," she recalled. "Of course the house was packed with all these illustrious celebrities like Steve Martin, Lorne, and every forgotten blues artist in the country, who had been dredged out of obscurity personally by Belushi and Danny."

According to Pat, Gilda's feelings that night were a mixture of self-effacement and a touch of professional jealousy—she, after all, had not yet danced on Broadway.

"She was embarrassed that she was getting so much attention from the crowd in the lobby. She felt it was John and Danny's night, and she didn't want to steal their limelight," Pat said. This was very characteristic of Gilda—always giving people what she called their "tribute."

"Gilda loved the show," Pat added. "She enjoyed it; it made her excited and happy. And I think it gave her the first glimmer that maybe she should have one of her own."

Indeed, that was soon to be in the works, and it would lead to a downturn in her career and the last upturn in her personal life.

By way of background, you have to know that Fred Silverman, then president of NBC, had set his sights on making Gilda into the new Lucille Ball. Of course it did not take a college degree in comedy to think of this. Gilda herself used to say:

"I never wanted to be a stand-up comic, because it's like being a knife thrower's assistant. You risk dying out there for a little applause. I love physical comedy. Women are getting into that again, since Lucy. Just give me that old conveyor belt and a lot of pies."

Any of Gilda's friends could have told you the same when she was still in high school. But to Silverman, "the man with the golden gut," also called "the maharajah of mediocrity," it was the greatest revelation of his life that Gilda could carry a prime-time comedy show. Moreover, he saw his own star hitched to Gilda's and thus inadvertently became the cause of her greatest show business failure, which coincided with his own fall from orbit.

Silverman was reported to be "obsessed" with getting Gilda her own prime-time variety/comedy series. As the "new Lucy," Gilda was going to be the vehicle to lift NBC out of third place and assure Silverman a permanent place in the sun.

According to Doug Hill and Jeff Weingrad, in their book *Saturday Night*, Silverman pitched the series idea to Lorne over Chinese food, in their first meeting in NBC's executive dining room, in August of 1978. Silverman envisioned a high-budget comedy/variety show along the lines of Carol Burnett's, airing live from nine to ten P.M. on Wednesday nights. Silverman even used to chant to his underlings, in the manner of a man behind a Shower Mike:

"Wednesday night at nine is Gilda time!"

Hill and Weingrad recount how during the next couple of months Gilda, Lorne, and Bernie Brillstein had a series of meetings about the series with NBC officials. Their objective was to structure a deal. The production budget was set at just under half a million dollars a show. Gilda would make around fifty thousand dollars a week. Gilda and Lorne would co-own the series. NBC offered a commitment to seventeen shows, thinking it would go on the air the following fall.

Gilda desperately wanted to do the series at first. She excitedly told her friends about it. She saw herself leaving "Saturday Night" or perhaps just making an occasional appearance, as Chevy Chase did. But then, suddenly, for reasons no one could really understand at the time, the project mysteriously petered out.

Averting her eyes in an uncharacteristic way, Gilda would only say she was "too tired," and that television had already "sucked enough of my blood" and that she wanted to take a rest.

Lorne explained to Hill and Weingrad that the show would "add five years to her TV sentence."

In October, Silverman asked Gilda and Lorne to come to his office to discuss the series. Silverman assumed it was still going ahead. Lorne did all the talking, Hill and Weingrad report, spending the whole meeting explaining why the show could not be done. The studio facilities stank, the censors would be a problem, the schedule was too complex, etc. Silverman was certain all the objections could be met. But to NBC executive Paul Klein, who was also at the meeting, it seemed as if Lorne was passing up the series on Gilda's behalf.

During the entire meeting Gilda sat, with her head down, in complete silence.

As Hill and Weingrad report, two weeks later Silverman

summoned Lorne to his office once more. He demanded a final decision on the series. Lorne was stunned, thinking he had already turned it down. Silverman could not comprehend Lorne's refusal, and he exploded. Lorne yelled back at him and stalked out.

Silverman later asked Mike Weinblatt, another NBC executive, to try to patch things up. Weinblatt met with Lorne and then Gilda in his office.

Gilda broke down in tears, saying she just could not do two shows and she did not want to break up the "Saturday Night" family.

However, soon afterward Gilda and Lorne embarked on the project that did just that—her Broadway show.

It was to be an old-fashioned Broadway revue. Even though it caused Gilda a great deal of grief, personally and professionally, it was one of those things that seemed like a good idea at the time.

Gilda was nobody's fool when it came to business, and she saw how much money and fame had flowed from the Blues Brothers juggernaut, with Belushi exclaiming at the top of his voice, "We're the best fucking band in the world!"

In the mirrored landscape of success and wealth beyond the dreams of ancient kings, it became clear that "Saturday Night" was not the end of the rainbow but merely a golden catapult to stardom that had lifted Chevy Chase, Dan Aykroyd, and John Belushi into uncharted orbits. Gilda felt she was next on the launching pad, and Lorne did too.

He was very particular about his recommendations to her. For instance, on Lorne's advice Gilda turned down an offer of $850,000 to costar with Robin Williams in the movie *Popeye.* Many of her other friends and I had advised her to take that job, but she turned it down because Lorne at the time had felt it would keep her from doing her best on "Saturday Night." It was the first time Gilda had not followed the advice of her old friends.

That Broadway revue had a modest enough genesis. Soon after the Blues Brothers record album came out, Gilda decided to make a record of her own, a cute little comedy album to be called *Gilda Radner, Live from New York*. It started out as something to fill the "SNL" Christmas hiatus. Gilda, Paul Shaffer, Michael O'Donoghue, and a few others from the show wrote some songs and musical sketches. Then Gilda invited Brooke Shields, me, and about 250 other people to crowd into the A&R recording studios on Seventh Avenue and Fifty-Second Street for the live taping.

There were quite a few things on that album that would never have gotten past the censors at NBC. Mike O'Donoghue's classic show opener, "Let's Talk Dirty to the Animals," was Gilda's special favorite.

Bill Murray brilliantly performed off-mike duties as master of ceremonies. He and Gilda were having a hot and heavy romance at the time, and, in what Hill and Weingrad call "a very touching spontaneous public display of affection and support," after the show he lifted her up and carried her offstage. All her friends thought it was a gas.

After the taping, which everyone enjoyed thoroughly, an insane whirlwind of business momentum suddenly picked up the album and flung it into the maelstrom.

Gilda said at the time that it was all an idea "just to make me some money."

But, for whatever reason, someone wanted to turn the album into a Broadway show, and someone else wanted to put it on a national tour, and then—hey, why not?—let's make the whole thing into a movie!

By deciding to make *Gilda Live* into a multimedia extravaganza, Gilda and the Brillstein-Michaels axis, inspired by the Blues Brothers, thought they would be able to run away from Fred Silverman and the "morticians," as Gilda called them, who ran NBC.

Gilda always used to describe them this way:

"You know, those guys whose eyes look like two television sets!"

The Broadway show did have the result of tearing Gilda away from "Saturday Night." Lorne also used it, according to Hill and Weingrad, as a vehicle to leave NBC for a time, to make feature films, and to start up Broadway Video, his production company. Gilda had said to NBC executives she did not want to break up the " 'Saturday Night' family." But if Lorne was leaving, and the Blues Brothers had gone their way, and Chevy was long gone, and Bill Murray was not far behind—well, the family was doing as many families do these days, going its separate ways.

But the departure from "Saturday Night" was not without its cost. First of all, it caused bad blood between Gilda and her dear old friend, John Belushi. According to Hill and Weingrad, John told Paul Shaffer and Bob Tischler, who had worked on the Blues Brothers show, not to get involved with Gilda.

"Just wait," Belushi told Shaffer. "We're doing the Blues Brothers [movie and tour], and we won't be coming back. I want you to be fresh. Just rest. Don't do the Gilda record."

John called Tischler to his "SNL" dressing room one night. When he arrived, John grabbed him and threw him against the wall and said,

"You're not doing the Gilda album! It's going to be a piece of shit!"

Shaffer and Tischler did not take John's green-eyed but accurate "advice." They remained coproducers of Gilda's album.

It was not deemed ready until June, more than five months after the taping. By then Lorne had already booked the Winter Garden Theater on Broadway for the month of August for the opening of Gilda's show.

On June 28, 1979, Gilda's thirty-third birthday, Paul Shaffer chartered a plane and flew to the Hamptons with the master tape. There was a small party at Lorne's place in Amagansett for the "premier listening." The tape was supposed to be Gilda's birthday present. Lorne's fiancée, Susan Forristal, served Gilda's favorite lunch, tuna fish salad, as all anxiously awaited Shaffer's arrival.

Shaffer came in looking as if he had not slept "for three days," according to Hill and Weingrad. All fortified their wine goblets and gathered around the tape recorder in Lorne's living room. Paul put on the tape.

Some reacted instantly; others just lapsed into stunned silence. According to Hill and Weingrad, it was clear to all that the tape was a disaster. They were listening to a modest little vaudeville act, with none of the power or pizzazz of the Blues Brothers or of "SNL" itself. It was one of those performances where "you had to be there." It was decided on the spot that the album could never be released.

Gilda left in tears, a "basket case." All by herself, disguised as a crotchety old lady with a horrible wig, she returned to New York.

In the same eventful summer of 1979, Gilda moved from Charles Street, in the Village, to the Windsor Hotel on Sixth Avenue and Fifty-Eighth Street. She had had two reasons: to be closer to her two jobs and for security. Now she had a third—to lock herself in her bedroom and cry without feeling totally alone.

"I grew up in a hotel," she said as she finished cleaning out her shelves on Charles Street. "I love living in hotels. You don't have to clean anything, they cook for you all night, and there's twenty-four-hour doorman, mail, and phone service."

Licking her wounds from the bitter disappointment of the record, she holed up in the hotel in a room that was almost entirely green. She spent much of the time in bed, watching television with a remote control. She felt the green color was therapeutic.

Her fondness for one-color schemes reflected the vibrations she needed at the time. Her solid-blue apartment on West Eighty-Fourth Street had been conducive to headiness, brilliant talk, and funny jokes. The green of her new place was better for healing, for meditation, for sulking.

Meanwhile, Lorne paced furiously, desperately trying to figure out a way to recoup the fortune he had sunk into this project, according to Hill and Weingrad. He decided the best defense was to attack: they would forge ahead with the Broadway show and record the album live on Broadway, acting almost as if nothing had happened. It did not take his considerable powers of persuasion to convince Gilda that was the right thing to do. By then she was totally unhinged, and if Lorne had asked her to put her hand in a fire she would merely have said, "Left or right?"

The show lurched toward opening night. Even by television standards the atmosphere was chaotic. According to Hill and Weingrad, the sets did not work, the writers fought with Lorne and each other (Michael O'Donoghue returned his *Gilda Live* jacket to Lorne, having first slashed the back with a knife), and there were arguments over publicity pictures and worries about slow ticket sales.

Through it all, true to her own star, Gilda did finally get her fondest wish—to tap-dance on Broadway.

Tap dancing was one of the highlights of her show, *Gilda Radner Live from New York*, at the Winter Garden Theater in 1979. Unfortunately, it was one of the few highlights of that disastrous episode.

The critics panned her show for the most part, not so much for lack of talent but because they felt the audience did not get its money's worth. They asserted that Gilda live on Broadway was more or less the same as Gilda live on "Saturday Night," with a few more swear words thrown in, and that it was not fair to charge $18.50 for a ticket to the same show you could watch for free on television. Because, as one columnist noted, "there is something about Gilda Radner that demands a hug," they tried to be kind.

Mel Gussow, in the nicest of the bad reviews, put it this way:

". . . Something crucial was missing. . . . Diehard Radnerians may be thoroughly entertained, but the evening does not take even adequate advantage of the star's talents. . . . Some of the sketches fall flat. . . . The material seems impoverished. . . . The show ends by making us wish for a bit of Weekend Update. . . . Unfortunately, her Broadway debut is a disappointment."

There was a handful of good reviews, in particular one by Clive Barnes in the *New York Post* that reflected my sentiments exactly:

"With her wrinkled-up face, snub-nose, and valiantly bushy-tailed grin, Gilda Radner is a different kind of charmer. But charmer she definitely is. . . . From the moment Miss Radner, displaying the most sublimely professional amateurism, bounces out on stage, beams a twenty-three-carat smile at the audience, and starts to sing the inspired and bawdy nonsense of 'Let's Talk Dirty to the Animals,' this depraved nymph has won us all."

Barnes went on: "Miss Radner can almost do everything, but is not really an actress but fundamentally a *shtick* artist. She plays funny people in a funny way—rather like, say, Peter Sellers. . . . The entire show is outrageously funny. There is scarcely a dull moment, and the swift evening is hip, flip and fresh. And as for the pocket Venus-sized dynamo, now Broadway's own Miss Radner, I doubt whether I could like anyone who didn't love her."

During this period Gilda was a nervous wreck, smoking twice as much as usual, eating huge quantities of food, and then spending bad quarter-hours in every bathroom on Broadway. She was so tired that in the middle of the run she fell sick and missed several performances. Now, with the tragedy of hindsight and the hindsight of tragedy, we can see that perhaps it was not all due to exhaustion, the official explanation.

Ticket sales finally picked up, and the show's run was extended for a few weeks into September. Personally, I enjoyed the show and saw it three times, but I did not pay for my tickets and was, as ever, loyal.

In spite of her inner turmoil, Gilda always received me warmly in her dressing room after the shows. Occasionally I would drop by without seeing the show, just to see her. At least this part, having her dressing room on Broadway, was her old childhood fantasy come true.

Her dressing table was cluttered with makeup and a jar of peanut butter. For the first time since I had known her, she also began to keep a bottle of vodka around. It helped calm her fears.

"The first few nights, I was so scared that I pretended I was just another girl in the show, and that it wasn't my responsibility," she said to the *New York Times.* "Lorne said, 'If you're not having a good time, no one else will. It's your show.' I began to realize that. . . . So now I have an act and can take it with me. It's like having a dress."

After each show, after the tears had dried, she walked across the empty stage in the silent theater by herself and, in a soft voice, sang "Sonny Boy." Gilda made it a practice to then hold court over a late dinner at Wally's, a show biz steak house on Forty-Ninth Street. As ever taking solace in food, in this hectic and stressful period, Gilda found relaxation only during these dinners. She never went home earlier than four in the morning, and she was always up early the next day, no dawdling. My wife and I sometimes joined her at Wally's, perhaps just for dessert, and Gilda invariably seemed as starved for a friendly face as for the food. She was already having a very hard time physically because of bulimia, but she kept tight control over the rest of her life—she never failed to be gracious and kind.

One night I brought a few of my California friends to her show, and we all joined her at Wally's for dinner afterward. Don Wright, Sandy Forrest, and Scot Morris were all fans of hers and beside themselves to be out to dinner with Gilda. She did her utmost to make them feel comfortable, and after a few minutes they were all talking and laughing with Gilda as if they had known one another for years.

Don recalls that night: "We were all sitting around this big round table, eating up a storm. I was sitting next to Gilda, and I was feeling very nervous, even though she was so gracious. I remember asking her this choked-up, nervous question, sounding to myself like a star-struck fan:

" 'Where do you get all this wonderful material?'

"She turned and stared at me with this sort of 'I-can't-believe-he-asked-me-that' look on her face, and she answered:

" 'I get it from my life!'

"I guess that's obvious, in a way. Of course you get it from your life. But her answer really stuck with me. It even inspired me years later when I was trying to figure out some design problem I had. This stuff comes outta you! Just like that gook in Roseanne Roseannadanna's eyes!"

A couple of weeks later, Sandy told me she had seen Gilda in the street, filming something. Gilda had stopped in the middle of her scene and gone over to Sandy to say hello. Sandy was very impressed by this unnecessary thoughtfulness, and Gilda told me shortly afterward:

"You know, those were really nice people you introduced me to the other night. That's a tribute to you."

In spite of her tribulations, in spite of the critics, she was in many respects very happy to be working on Broadway. In spite of it all, she was in her element, she was out of the maw of television, and she had gotten one of her fondest wishes. But bad reviews close shows.

Unfortunately, the "bad review" feeling also prevailed back on the seventeenth floor of Rockefeller Center, where *Gilda Live* was considered a rip-off of "Saturday Night." There was also resentment of the amount of time Lorne was spending with Gilda. One writer called it the "teacher's pet syndrome."

Even Bill Murray came to hate Gilda's show. He would tell "SNL" people, "You're not working here anymore. You're working on Gilda's shit." Their romance began to fall apart, which only increased the pressure on Gilda.

When the show closed, after four weeks of cheering audiences and mixed reviews, Gilda suddenly found herself looking forward to nothing, neither Broadway nor television nor boyfriend.

Gilda's record came out as a Warner Brothers release in October 1979. The movie finally came out in March 1980. Both bombed.

Gilda later looked back on all this in a grandly philosophical way. As she described it in *It's Always Something*:

"When *Gilda Live* opened . . . in 1979, the morning paper had a review with a headline that said, 'Gilda Radner Has No Talent—Zip, Zilch, Zero.' Show business is a gamble. There is no certainty."

9

The Death of John Belushi

"We always expected this to happen"

AFTER LIVING IN THE WINDSOR HOTEL FOR SEVERAL MONTHS, when her head was finally cooled out and she had more or less forgotten the show, movie, and record debacles, Gilda moved again, this time to a white-and-wood color scheme in the legendary Dakota Apartments, at the corner of Seventy Second Street and Central Park West.

Always the astute businesswoman, and following her brother Michael's advice, Gilda had bought a splendid parlor-floor-through apartment in the famous building for a mere $150,000.

"It was a steal," she said, in her best Roseanne voice, echoing the most popular contemporary expression of New York real estate mavens.

To Gilda, always a sucker for newer and better ways to consecrate food, the chief feature of her Dakota apartment was its genuine industrial-strength kitchen, complete with a twelve-burner professional restaurant stove and stainless-steel built-in wall-sized refrigerator and freezer. She could now keep a couple of cows in her apartment and have room left over. The fact that she barely knew how to cook did not stop her at all.

After moving to the Dakota, Gilda entered another phase of her life. She was all ready to begin a "life after television" as the Broadway bombshell or, in the words of the media, "America's Sweetheart."

First, becoming a sweetheart in reality as well as name, she reaped another great positive benefit from *Gilda Live.* Gilda fell in love with G. E. Smith, the cool, sexy bandleader on *Gilda Live* and now on "Saturday Night."

Kitty was the hostess, and Eric roasted suckling pigs when Gilda celebrated her "secret engagement party" at the Shelter Island Beach Club in the summer of 1980.

It was the social event of the season. Dozens of people showed up on sailboats. Anne Beatts came in a fast launch. One person, Jim Signorelli of "Saturday Night," landed in a seaplane. Lorne helped Eric take care of the music, saying, "It's better to have no music than bad music."

The big secret of the evening was that Gilda's engagement to G. E. Smith had taken place there earlier that day. It remained a secret to all but a chosen few. Most thought it was just a "summer's end" party on the beach.

For just about the second time in her life, Gilda was happy and in love. She danced with G.E. on the balcony of the beach club. She and I danced. It was a beautiful scene on a warm summer night with the sky full of the Milky Way, an infinity of stars streaming in a nothingness of twinkles. She was quiet that night, just content to smile and dance and eat and smile some more.

In the Indian summer of 1980, Gilda married G.E.

They had a civil ceremony in downtown Manhattan. Gilda wore a crinoline on her head and carried a bouquet of lollipops. G.E. wore his best jeans. They went to live in Gilda's apartment in the Dakota.

Like the engagement, her marriage to G.E. took place in

secret. The first official announcement came in September, when Gilda invited me to her wedding party, to be held at an old school gymnasium, of all places, on Varick Street, between the Village and SoHo.

The school was decorated like a teenage prom hall. Gilda chartered a school bus to bring anyone who lived uptown. Kitty catered hot dogs, potato chips, M&M's, popcorn, brownies, chocolate chip cookies, Cokes, and other assorted junk foods. The band played fifties and sixties rock and roll. Gilda wore pants and was very happy.

More than anything, I wanted to dance with her. Although I am a pretty good athlete, for some reason I have never "learned" any dance steps, so I do not consider myself a great dancer until I get at least four drinks in me. That evening, since I was walking and not driving, I had imbibed the inevitable and was really trying to rise to the occasion.

Gilda, of course, was a superb dancer, and the last thing I wanted to do was drag her down.

But I choked up. I took her hands to a fast tune, and suddenly my old high school dance fears resurfaced, like an old case of angina pectoris. I could not dance a step.

Gilda instantly understood my predicament. She saved the day.

"Do t'ai chi," she said.

Of course! I'd been practicing t'ai chi for years. I just never thought of it in relation to dancing. It's a martial art, but dancing looks sort of like a martial art, doesn't it? Maybe that's the secret connection I'd missed all these years. All those dances, all those beautiful women lost because I forgot to do t'ai chi and thought I had to do some kind of American Bandstanding! This was a painful revelation to a guy who really thought he was going to cut a dash on Broadway.

"Do t'ai chi!" And it worked! Instantaneously Gilda

transformed me into a terrific dancer as we did t'ai chi together.

I Grasped the Bird's Tail, she spun around. I did Purple Swallow Opens the Scissors, and she did something very close to Pat the High Horse. Dancing is just natural, I discover. Dancing is just the same body—two arms, two legs, two eyes, a nose, and a mouth. I had to make sure not to break her arm, but otherwise it worked perfectly. I had really had a breakthrough in dancing.

According to *Rolling Stone*, this was *the* party of 1980. The mag noted, "Gilda keeps NY humming by the bash of the year . . . sock hop . . . crepe paper decorations . . . surprise marriage . . . rampant heavy petting. . . ."

Well, it sure was a great party for me. It was not the fanciest, but it was the best. It was the one where Gilda taught me how to dance.

In the same autumn of 1980, Gilda again teamed up with Mike Nichols, who had directed her and Sam Waterston in Jean Kerr's comedy *Lunch Hour.* That play opened on Broadway on November 12, to good reviews. Three days later "Saturday Night Live," began its sixth season, with a completely new cast and a new executive producer, a friend of Woody Allen's named Jean Doumanian. Those reviews were terrible. Friends and the world at large attributed it primarily to the fact that Gilda and the other originals had left the fold for good.

Gilda seemed reasonably happy after her marriage to G.E. It was a tough, weird, chaotic time in the outside world, though, and their high-profile bohemian lifestyles soon felt like millstones instead of rocket launchers. Shortly after G.E. moved into the Dakota, in the winter of 1980, John Lennon was shot while standing in front of the building.

G.E. and Gilda held each other tight that night, she wrote.

Immediately, all the celebrities in New York became extremely nervous. Belushi began to travel and train with Bill "Superfoot" Wallace, the world karate champion. A week or so after Lennon's murder, Gilda came over to my apartment on Perry Street for dinner. She was driven in a limo by her newest companion—a professional bodyguard, an anvil-armed, seven-foot-tall leg breaker named Walter.

Always at heart the simplest and kindest of mortals, Gilda begged my wife to let Walter come upstairs and eat dinner with us, rather than having him wait outside in the car.

Of course we agreed, and he turned out to be a likable and very reassuring companion. For the record, that night we ate corn soup and shrimp diablo. Gilda loved the meal, as did Walter.

In March 1982, when John Belushi died in spite of his karate training and twenty-four-hour guard, Gilda felt confirmed in her new reclusiveness.

Her reaction to Belushi's death was almost like "I knew it." She was saddened but not shocked.

She said:

"The truth is that since everything he did in his life was so suicidal, his death did not really surprise me. We always expected this to happen."

One must mention here the amazing "backwardly prophetic" film made for "Saturday Night" by Tom Schiller, called *Don't Look Back in Anger.* In it John Belushi, as an old man, visits the graves of all the other "Saturday Night" stars.

> JOHN: (*Approaching the graveyard*) They all thought I'd be the first to go. I was one of those live-fast die-young real-good-looking-corpse types, you know. But I guess they were wrong. There they are, all of my friends. This is

> the Not Ready for Prime Time Cemetery. Come on up. . . .
>
> Here's Gilda Radner. She had her own show on Canadian television for years and years, the "Gilda Radner Show." Well, at least now I can see her on reruns. Cute as a button, God bless her.

Letting death be her adviser, Gilda let Belushi's death drive her further out of what she saw as the unhealthy maelstrom of New York media life. In spite of having moved into the Dakota a relatively short time before, she decided once more it was time to move to the country and perhaps indulge a small part of that old fantasy of having a farm. She bought a beautiful two-century-old stone farmhouse on Scofieldtown Road in Stamford, Connecticut.

In the career department, Gilda began to concentrate on films as the way to move along as a comedian. On several occasions she described herself as bone-tired and feeling overexposed on the world of television.

"They suck your blood," she said again of TV.

Occasionally Gilda would watch a rerun of herself on TV. Once she said:

"When I watch myself on 'Saturday Night,' I go back to the mood I was in that week. If I was in love, I feel in love again. If I was having my period, my period comes again! Whatever I was going through at the time."

Around this time, just before getting together with Gene Wilder, Gilda began to worry that perhaps she was just a "one-show actress," the same way Lorne worried that he might be a "one-show producer."

She was a very fine actress, as well as a clown, and she knew this. Feeling she was being underused as an actress, she asked me to write something for her. In most correct Liggett School style, she even suggested the perfect theme and format.

Quoting Lorne, she told me:

"You know, no one has ever written the definitive work on unrequited love. I want to play in one of those *French* movies, one of those charming little comedies."

I could really see Gilda in "one of those *French* movies," so I went to work. An expert on unrequited love myself, I wrote a treatment based on our experiences in Europe. A few weeks later I asked her to read my treatment, *Traveling Companions.*

A week or so later she told me that she had read it and liked it.

"I want to send it to Bernie," she said, meaning her agent and manager, Bernie Brillstein. She did so.

Bernie thought it was "too soft."

"They want movies like *Midnight Express* now," Bernie said.

I tried to imagine Gilda in a movie like *Midnight Express*, even a comic version. That treatment remains to be written.

Her first movie, also in 1980, was *First Family*, Buck Henry's political satire. It also starred Bob Newhart and Madeline Kahn. Gilda played the president's daughter. It was generally considered a disaster.

She then made two films with Gene Wilder, *Hanky Panky* and *The Woman in Red.* Along with a third Wilder film, *Haunted Honeymoon*, they pretty much bombed, although *The Woman in Red* was merely a disappointment, not a total floperoo.

For Gilda, as she has written, *Hanky Panky* was the greatest moment of her life. She finally met her true love, Gene Wilder. She arranged a quick, quiet, friendly divorce with G. E. Smith. And she began to look for a new method of continuing her artistic career.

For some unfortunate reason the films she worked on, with or without Gene, were poor vehicles for her talent, as had been *Broadway*, and as had been *Gilda Live* if you believed the negative critics. One should note that this need to find ever-newer "vehicles" is largely a function of modern times. George Burns survived for more than fifty years with just twelve minutes of material. Only the insatiable monster of modern show business requires that performers keep "changing their acts" every few months, weeks, even days.

After meeting Gene and falling in love, Gilda's career did not seem to matter to her anymore. She consciously and happily went into semiseclusion, spending time in her farmhouse in Connecticut and at Gene's mansion in Bel Air. Even if she didn't have a job, at least she was finally, madly in love, as she has described in an incomparable manner in her book.

Kitty reminisces about a visit to Connecticut during this period, after Gilda and Gene were together.

"I got there on a Saturday evening. When we woke up on Sunday morning, Gilda spent the whole morning on the phone with her family and friends. She called everyone she knew in Detroit, people in California. She spent hours doing that. She talked to her cousins. She even talked to her mom. Then she took me across the road to meet these people who took care of her house when she was gone. She was very sweet to them and spent lots of her private time with them.

"She was getting very into exercise then too. She spent one hour doing exercises from this videotape. It was not Jane Fonda; I forget what it was. But she had been doing them for a long time. I think she wanted to be in shape for Gene, because he liked to play tennis and stuff. Anyway, she liked it because she could do them to music. She was still working at singing, tap dancing, and all her stage stuff. I think at that point she didn't care if she had an audience of one million or just one.

"She also used to visit Dibby in Hamilton a lot in those days, 'cause Dibby was not feeling too well and Gilda couldn't stand the idea that she might be hurting."

Meanwhile, the movie and television industry began to ask, "What happened to Gilda?"

From a professional standpoint what happened was, so that she could hang out with Gene, on or off location, she began to write. From a personal standpoint, Gilda had found the love of her life.

10

Gilda in Love

"My boyfriend's a movie star"

Before Gene, it was with heart-rending awareness of her inner suffering that over the years we watched Gilda go through her long-running series of inappropriate and sometimes painful love affairs.

They did not always have comic turns, but one that did was the one involving yours truly. It is an episode Gilda herself named:

"Saved by the Bell."

When Gilda was still living on Eighty-Fourth and Riverside, in the mid-seventies, things began to get steamy between us one winter night. As I indicated earlier, I had always had a thing for Gilda, but the way I saw it, the time had never been right, the circumstances had never been right.

I had been sleeping in the living room. But that night I was feeling cold and lonely, and I asked her if I could sleep next to her, in her bed.

"As long as you don't try nothin'," she said, laughing, psychic as always. I laughed too.

I walked into her bedroom. Her closet doors were open, revealing her astounding wardrobe. All her clothes were from Bendel or Bonwit's. She took very good care of them, and they were all neatly arranged by color, with matching shoes underneath. No matter how crazy her outer life got, her closet was always like this—immaculate, in order. When she no longer wanted to wear something, she would give it to Kitty, who was still a size eight when Gilda had gotten down to a size two. Even though Gilda had all these clothes and never changed clothes fewer than fifty times a day, she always managed to look like she had just thrown something on.

So we were in her bedroom. It smelled of clean gold satin sheets and bubble gum. I was sitting on her bed. She was wearing a pink nightgown. Her hair was hanging down, surrounding her sweet, small face in a softly bushy tangle.

My voice suddenly became husky.

She said she had never thought of me that way before. I'm not entirely sure I believed her.

"If you're gonna get sexy, I'm gonna get smart," she quipped in that "funny" tone of voice she had mastered.

"I'm feeling sexy," I said.

"And I'm feeling smart," she replied.

"Listen, Dave," she told me in a very soft, kind voice. "Sex is lovely. It can be so great. But you know how it is. You do it with someone and everything changes. A few days, or a few weeks, or a few months later, you hate each other. I don't know why that is. It's such a lovely thing—but do we dare risk ruining what we have?"

Even in my rapidly tumescing state I was strangely moved and recognized the truth and beauty of what she was saying. But I was horny as the devil, and I persisted, talking through my schlong.

"But I just had a terrible time with a magician," Gilda

confessed, changing tacks suddenly in a spirited defense of her honor.

"What do you mean?" I asked, unable to restrain my curiosity.

She told me that she had recently gone out with Doug Henning and was totally charmed. And then, as she put it:

"I let him touch me with his magic wand, but then *he* disappeared."

I pressed, insisting I was no low-life swine like Doug Henning—and that I was a better magician too.

Apparently, somewhere along the way, I said the right thing. Suddenly something happened to the atmosphere in the room. It changed color and smell and got real twinkly, and Gilda began to melt. She was basically a warmhearted girl, after all.

Just as she started to relax, the phone rang. She always kept a phone right by her bed.

"Saved by the bell," she said with a laugh, and she answered.

"Hello," she said cheerfully.

"Sure," she added, "just a minute." Oh, damn, I thought to myself—some kind of blasted delay.

She handed the phone to me.

"It's for you," she said with a large and wicked grin.

It was my girlfriend, Liza, calling from California. I had completely forgotten about her.

Gilda had always criticized Liza as being "too strict," but she had nothing to complain about in her strictly uncanny sense of timing.

After a strained telephone conversation I hung up and tried to get back to where I was with Gilda. But the damned telephone call had thrown me off my stride in a major way. So I said a really politically incorrect thing. Overcome by mad lust, I mentioned my *zezi*.

"Why are men so into the size of their . . . their . . .

things?" she wanted to know with that frowning grimace that brings out the musical staff in her forehead. I could see I had displeased her.

"We're very attached," I said, knowing a joke would get her back on track.

She laughed.

"Don't worry, Dave. One day, when we're both fifty, we'll get married, or have sex, or something," she said kindly, and I really believed her. We kissed good night, tenderly, with real love, and went to sleep.

Months later, when another writer did a magazine profile on her, she told me he had the biggest *zezi* she never saw.

"But he was gay," she said, laughing.

I am not going to go into a catalog of Gilda's affairs, other than to characterize her love philosophy using an old epigram of my grandfather's: "When you go on a spree, go the whole hog, including the postage!"

Dennis Grimaldi notes that during the "mid-show" period Gilda was madly in love with several men at once. She had not yet entirely gotten over Bill Murray. She had had the fling with Chris Sarandon. She was going out with Kevin Kline. And in addition, all this time, says Dennis, "she was secretly and desperately in love with—Lorne!"

In the late seventies Gilda acquired a sort of live-in private male secretary or, as we described him, "her fag." We pretended we were using the word in the English public school sense, but of course it was really the American sense. In general, homosexuality repelled Gilda. She once said to me, "How can they stand it? Fuckin' the fudge every night! Yecchhh!"

Nevertheless, in those days every big female star hired a gay man to call her own and do her bidding. Gilda's was named Dale, and he functioned as her executive secretary, gofer, and quartermaster general.

Originally from Palm Beach, Dale was a snippy type but a decent sort at heart. He really tried to look out for Gilda's welfare, although there was a faction that felt he improved a room by leaving it. Few of Gilda's friends and colleagues trusted him, and sometimes conversation would stop dead when he came in.

Gilda, however, trusted him implicitly. He ate out of her hand. As far as I know, he was always loyal to her and trustworthy beyond a doubt. He was also very honest with her. When she was crying one day about her miserable, tormented, tempestuous love life, Dale made a very telling observation.

"Gilda," he chirruped, "your problem is . . . you shit where you eat!"

And vice versa.

I realized she was going through one of these awful affairs in the year 1977, as I was performing one of the aforementioned magic shows for the "SNL" cast. I did a mind-reading trick in which I "psychically" read a sealed message Gilda had written and then burned to cinders.

Her message was "Torment."

Later that night Gilda revealed to me she was madly and unfortunately in love with a well-known filmmaker. He was a junkie, she said, and she knew she had gotten too deeply involved with him and felt she was stepping to the edge of the abyss.

She had a date with him that night. I went home.

At three o'clock in the morning, Gilda called me up, crazy to go out to eat.

"Let's go to Sandolino's," she said, naming a diner in the Village. "I love that place. They're open all night."

We went. She told me the sad tale of her evening, the

lowest she had ever had, the worst night of her life.

She had waited for him in her apartment on Charles Street until one A.M. He failed to show up. Finally, after one, he called and told her he'd been sidetracked.

Gilda was crushed as she told me what he had said:

"He had to stop off to get a blow job from a hooker!"

She began to cry.

"I hate it here," she sniffled. "I hate New York. You could be dead in the bathroom, and no one would ever find you."

I could only nod agreement and sigh.

"Thank God for this food," she said, eating to come down from a bad trip, even though she was not stoned at all. "Sometimes it's the only pleasure I have in life."

She ate like a horse, then went to throw up. She came back as if nothing had happened. But I knew, and she knew I knew. We continued eating until five A.M., ordering just about everything on the menu. She ate four meals for herself and half of mine. She made four-and-a-half trips to the bathroom.

I offered to kill the filmmaker, but she said no.

"He's like a drug," Gilda said. "I gotta have more."

As she moved through her early to mid-thirties, Gilda began to hear her inner clock ticking loudly, unaware that it was a time bomb. Her career and her aching heart began to conflict.

"I'm doing great on the show, but if I don't have someone to talk baby talk with, it all seems worthless," she said. She really needed someone to laugh with. For her Broadway show she wrote a touching song about a boy she used to kiss (with her clothes on) while listening to *The Two Thousand Year Old Man.*

"Pretty soon," she said in this period, "I'll be over thirty-five, and I'll have to find a man who's willing to father my mongoloid children."

After she finally screwed up the courage to go cold turkey with the filmmaker, she thought she had really found her permanent baby-talk companion in the actor Ben Masters.

Benny and Gilda had a long and sweet romance that she tried mightily to move onto the marriage altar. They lived together happily for more than a year on Charles Street, and most of us thought this was really it, true love at last.

Unfortunately, Gilda and Benny ran into existential problems. They loved each other, but they couldn't keep it together.

Ben convinced me of his feeling for her the day he coined a phrase that has since passed into the language in somewhat different form. Speaking of his love for Gilda, he said:

"I'd drag my ass through broken glass just to catch the reflection of her pussy in a mud puddle!"

But in those late seventies, Gilda's star was rising and Ben's was staying more or less in place. He became uncomfortable being Mr. Gilda Radner, and eventually Gilda realized that no matter how many "ordinary" men she liked, the difference in their domains would dominate the relationship. Even if Gilda could get past it, the guy, in this case Benny, could not.

She realized she would have to marry someone of her own station.

Ben backed off with a double dose of the yips: not only was he cowed by her success; he also felt trapped by Gilda's overwhelming neediness. That part was right out of the women's magazines: "men that won't commit and the women who love them too much."

On this account Gilda sometimes fell into the depths of despair over Benny. I tried to comfort her.

"Gilda, don't worry," I said. "You're a beautiful, desirable, charming woman. You'll find your true love for sure."

Gilda shook her head and summed up her complex relationship with Benny in one devastatingly perceptive statement.

"The problem is that I'm a man," she lamented in reply. "I'm not a woman. I'm a man."

All of this somehow goes toward explaining why Gene Wilder ultimately became the perfect man for Gilda.

In between Benny and Gene, Gilda's affair with Bill Murray flashed off and on for a long time, beginning in the seventies and not ending until her Broadway show in 1980. It was interspersed with small summer romances with stars like Elliott Gould and Paul Simon on her part and don't-get-me-started on his.

Gilda and Billy had true affection for each other, and he seemed at least to be of the right stature and sensibility for her. For better or worse, though, Billy was a great womanizer, and Gilda—like legions of other women—eventually saw it would be hard to land him permanently.

Bill Murray is a genuine Great and Loyal American, one of the few who actually ended up marrying his true love, his childhood sweetheart, Mickey Kelly. But before that, his womanizing became the subject of many underground legends, and considerable envy, on all coasts of the known world.

There is a fellow from Los Angeles, for instance, who shall remain nameless. He was having a lot of trouble with his marriage. Finally, in a desperate attempt to put some zing back into their lives, he invited his wife on a second honeymoon at one of America's famous western resorts.

It was perfect. The suite was elegant. The view was splendid. There were fresh flowers in each room and bowls of beautiful fruits. They spent the day walking in the woods and holding hands on the beach. That night they had champagne, and they were beginning to feel the old stir that had attracted them in the first place. With rekindled love in their eyes, they retired to bed.

The man made his move, and just as he was beginning to warm his wife up, they became aware of ever-increasing sounds from the suite next door.

This is a thick-walled resort hotel, mind you, so the sounds from next door must have been ear-shattering in person. They were already coming through the walls at a high decibel level, and they were the sounds of what the man described quite honestly as "the wildest fucking I had ever heard or even heard about. They were like two wild animals in there. It was violent. It was wet. I expected blood to come spurting through the walls, along with a waterfall of sperm and love juice. They screamed; they bellowed. And then, when it was over, they groaned for a few minutes and started all over again!"

This went on all night. Needless to say, the feeble approaches of our lovelorn couple quickly wilted. God knows what the wife was thinking, but the husband—now ex-husband—is sure she wanted nothing more than to costar in the next-door production.

The next morning, the man stepped out into the hall of the hotel. Simultaneously the door opened next to him, and you already have guessed who came out. It was none other than Bill Murray. He was wearing one of his goofy grins, and he said,

"Hey, pardner."

To this day the man cannot stay in the same room in

which someone has mentioned Bill Murray. He never goes to his movies, wishes he had not seen *Ghostbusters*, and blames lucky, lovely Billy for ruining his life.

Billy did not ruin Gilda's life—if anything they enriched each other's life. But ultimately, he ended up marrying his true love and Gilda hers.

When Gilda threw my wedding reception in her Charles Street home in 1979, my beautiful bride and I already knew she was secretly suffering from a form of jealousy. In keeping with the road not taken throughout her life, she had always wanted a normal, traditional existence with husband and children. She used to hide this with a joke:

"I can't even take care of a plant. What would I do with my kids?"

The day before the wedding, she took all her valuables out and stashed them in a hotel room. The shelves, which had been full of mementos, books, and tchotchkes, were practically empty except for flowers. During the party she joked to me:

"They must be saying 'Gee, Miss Radner lives a very spare life, doesn't she?'"

Since many of the guests were fellow journalists and other disreputable sorts, I felt she was a bit worried that this private bash would show up in the papers somewhere. In certain circles it was considered "the social event of the season." People I did not really want to invite begged me for an invitation. I knew it was not because they wanted to be at my wedding but because they knew it was at Gilda's house and there was always the off chance that they might get to screw a starlet or two. There were a few other "names" there, besides Gilda, and in fact a few crashers did manage to penetrate our defenses. Every once in a while I still meet someone I have never seen before who tells me, "Oh, I was at your wedding party!" I wasn't about to throw them out, and neither was she, so surely she had been right to protect the heirlooms.

Gilda made very sure not to steal the limelight from my bride, Isa. Our hostess wore very dowdy clothes and a little red bonnet that made her look really ugly.

After we were married, when Isa was pregnant with our daughter, Gilda told us, very seriously:

"Being famous can make you afraid to have children. I didn't become famous until I was thirty years old. Growing up is hard enough without having to live up to the expectations that go along with fame."

She was thinking of her relations with her father, no doubt, and wondering if her child would miss out on anonymity and the freedom to observe without being observed—the secret to her comedy and characters.

Even though she sometimes said all this as a way of justifying not having children, we saw the lady doth protest too much. As she confirms in her book, she pined for the love and family happiness that eluded her until near the very end and then eluded her forever. In any case, when my daughter, Karina, was born, Gilda gave her a really nifty playpen.

After we had our second child, Sam, Gilda wrote me a letter in which she advised, plaintively:

"Take care of your tiny family. It's the most important of all."

Motherhood eluded Gilda, but she at least was able to choose godmotherhood. She became godmother to Alan Zweibel's three kids and to Kitty's Ryan and Isabel. She asked Kitty:

"Are you sure I can be a godmother if I'm not Catholic?"

Kitty assured her it was OK.

"Well, what am I supposed to do? What do godmothers do?" Godmothering is not a *yiddische naches.*

Kitty said, well, you just be nice to the kids, and give them presents once in a while, and answer all their questions, and let them know they can rely on you in a pinch.

"Oh," Gilda said, relieved. "Good. I thought you had to get circumcised or something."

She made Ryan a lovely needlepoint in a yellow frame. By the time Isabel was born, though, she was not feeling well enough to make anything.

No one can write more beautifully than Gilda has about her romance with Gene Wilder. But one interesting tale, a footnote to the classic love story she related in her book, is the story of how Gilda wooed and won Gene.

It came about largely because of our mutual friend, that keen observer of life and love, Pat O'Donoghue.

As you remember, Pat was another old crony from Ann Arbor, Gilda's date for the Blues Brothers concert. At the time Gilda ran off with Jeff Rubinoff, she had been subletting Pat's apartment on Monroe Street. Pat's life is worth a book all by itself, but suffice it to say that after a tumultuous marriage to Tom Copi, the jazz photographer, she fell in love with and married Bruce Jay Friedman, the author of such classics as *The Lonely Guy's Book of Life* and the screenplay to *Stir Crazy,* starring Gene Wilder and Richard Pryor.

Gilda and Pat had bonded quickly toward the end of Gilda's college career. The common theme once again was food: Pat and Gilda's mutual friend Kitty was learning how to cook, and the smell drew both of them at many mealtimes.

"At that time Gilda was madly in love with that guy Rick,

I think his name was, and that was the first time I'd seen her in love," Pat said, mentioning an ex-boyfriend that I think was Rick Ayers but Pat says is someone else. "I saw right then that when she was in love, nothing else really mattered. She went the whole hog."

Including the postage.

During Gilda's years in Canada, O'D went to California, and they fell out of touch. But when Gilda came to New York to do "Saturday Night," she ran into Pat in the Village, and "we instantly picked up and continued our unique friendship, as if we had been apart for only a few days," Pat recalls.

Pat eventually moved into our Village compound, taking over Kitty and Eric's apartment at 31 Bank Street, right around the corner from Gilda, the Belushis, Schiller, and me.

"We could always talk to each other on the same intimate level, even if we hadn't seen each other for years," she adds, confirming again Gilda's remarkable ability to make everyone feel special in her presence, raising the low and lowering the high to meet exactly at heart level.

From hanging around the set of *Stir Crazy*, Pat knew Gene Wilder before Gilda began to work on *Hanky Panky* with him in August 1981.

"I thought he was kind of weird," Pat said. "He's just like in the movies—kind of moony-eyed and goony and I guess rather sweet. He shakes your hand, then holds on to it while looking soulfully into your eyes. He fancies himself some kind of writer too, and that kind of hacked me off. He wanted to write the sequel to *Stir Crazy*, so I was jealous because I considered he was taking bread out of our mouths. So I told Gilda to watch out for him. But the next thing I hear, they're renting a house in the Hamptons, she's madly in love with him. They're not married yet, and then she asks me for advice on how to land him, based on how I landed Bruce.

"What I told her was completely alien to her nature: patience. I never insisted on Bruce's marrying me. We dated for three years, and Gilda used to call me in amazement, saying, 'How can you stand it? He has grown children!'

"Once, right after Bruce and I started getting real serious, Gilda was thrilled and mentioned it to Laraine Newman. Laraine said, 'But wait a minute; I heard he was going out with Diane.'

"Gilda relayed that to me, and I just put it out of my mind. So she used to say to me, 'How can you stay so calm? How can you stand it?'

"And I just told her, 'Listen, I love him. That's it. If it works, it works. I give it two years. If we're not living together after two years, well. . . .'

"Gilda soon saw it *was* working with us, and she asked me for advice on how to be patient. She heard the clock ticking—Gene was a lot older than she.

"I just told her, 'Be cool and concentrate on other things.' Gilda really tried to do so."

In the winter of 1982, Gilda divorced G.E. "Then a very good thing happened," O'D continued. "Gene built a tennis court and a wine cellar in her Connecticut house. That made her a lot less insecure. It was sort of like an engagement ring. For a brief moment there, she was truly, finally happy."

They were finally living together in the summer of 1982, when Gene took Gilda back to France. Gene is a great Francophile, and this time, thank God, Gilda had a wonderful time. She learned to appreciate "the difference," as she called it, and, with Gene, Gilda learned the world could be a pleasure and she could love it.

On September 18, 1984, Gilda and Gene got married in a small village in the south of France. They were blissfully happy for two years, which Gilda has described in detail in her book. All I can add is an extract from a letter she wrote me just before her marriage:

"Well, I made it to thirty-seven years of age, and I'm not doing too badly. I'm searching around a lot for a life outside of show business where things go slower and seem more real. I spend a lot of time traveling, and now I like Paris and I'm not afraid of the difference.

"My boyfriend's a movie star, and I want to be a writer so I can take my work with me wherever he goes. I have a wee, tiny dog named Sparkle that I take with me whever [*sic*] I go.

"I avoid New York because it hurts my guts.

"I'm not going to change the word whever [*sic*] 'cause it's too hot today. . . ."

"Dave, thanks for remembering my birthday and . . . thanks again for saving my life so I could get to right now which is the best it's been in a long time. . . ."

Gilda was thrilled with the notion of being a writer/wife. It satisfied both sides of her moonchild nature.

After Gene and Gilda were married, Pat was nursing her new baby, Molly, when she saw Gilda on TV promoting *Roseanne Roseannadanna's "Hey, Get Back to Work!" Book*, which she had written with Alan Zweibel in 1983. Pat called her and informed her she was a new mom. Gilda got very excited and told Pat she was trying to get pregnant too.

"Did you smoke while you were pregnant?" Gilda asked.

"Yes, a little," Pat admitted.

"Oh, good," Gilda said, "so I'm gonna keep smoking too."

For months Gilda plied Pat with questions about children. "She wanted to know everything about babies," Pat said. "So I kept sending her pictures, notes, all the little details only a mother can love. Eventually, though, I realized she was having trouble getting pregnant, so I stopped sending the pictures."

Gilda has written heartbreakingly about the pain of this period, when she and Gene desperately tried to have a child. She already suspected there was something terribly wrong with her.

11

" 'Bunny! Bunny!' Doesn't Work"

"Thanks for the love for all these years"

WE HAVE FOLLOWED GILDA'S LIFE MORE OR LESS CHRONOlogically, and as night follows day, finally we come to the shocking, screaming, cosmically unjust, objectively tragic climax, a part that is extremely difficult for me to write about or even think about at all.

Gilda covered this ground in a brilliant, moving way in her own memoir, describing how in a cruelly ironic twist of fate she finally found love but could neither enjoy it nor bear its fruits. Her description of her love affair with Gene Wilder, then the tragedy that took bliss from her grasp just as she was learning what it felt like, will surely go down as one of the bravest, wisest, wittiest, most disturbing pieces of writing of all time.

As Gilda wrote: ". . . I've learned the hard way that some poems don't rhyme, and some stories don't have a clear beginning, middle and end."

I can add very little to Gilda's own words and can say next to nothing about her all-too-clear end, except to tell a couple of funny and a couple of sad stories as I know they happened. Those who haven't already done so may wish to read her book *It's Always Something.*

Incidentally, she did not see the hardbound copy of her book until just one week before she died. In the paperback edition of Gilda's book, Gene has added two electrifying elements, found posthumously, that did not appear in the original. One is called "Right Hand Questions—Left Hand Answers." It's a meditation on her cancer, with Gilda's questions written by her right hand and answers apparently by her left. Among other entries, there is one "right-hand question" that is chilling:

> Is cancer your mother inside you?

Her "left-hand answer" is even more disturbing as it brings her life full circle:

> She doesn't want me to exist.

In 1986 Gilda was finally diagnosed with cancer, as she had feared all her life. Her old world fell away as she entered the instinct-bending hell of hospitals. Gilda became painfully aware of the truth of the old Jewish proverb: "God has put two kinds of doctors on earth: those who help you die and those who prevent you from living."

Pat O'Donoghue and most other friends did not know about her illness at this point. But all became aware of the huge vacuum created by Gilda's absence from our lives.

"Suddenly," Pat recalled, "Gilda started spending a lot of time traveling, a lot of time in California. She dropped out of touch with everybody in New York, all her old crowd. I figured it was just her extended honeymoon with Gene, because you know Gilda—when she's in love, there's nothing else in the world."

But Pat soon became aware of the real reason through the newspapers:

"Suddenly, like a lot of her old friends, I read about her disease in the *National Enquirer*."

During the same "darkening of the light" period near the end of her life, I had known Gilda was having health problems, but as soon as I heard she was feeling unwell, she would bounce back again. Like Pat, I did not see much of Gilda in these last days, since Isa and I were raising our children in New York and she was spending a great deal of time in California and France, with Gene and his friends, until she became too ill to travel. We corresponded and kept in touch by telephone, but every time we made contact Gilda invariably minimized her ill health. She describes in the book how, during this period, beginning in 1985, her doctors continually pooh-poohed her fears that she had cancer, and she did not want to seem delicate, cranky, or burdensome to her friends.

When I saw the *National Enquirer* headline in the checkout line at the store, I too was stunned. But I was well aware of the penchant of the *Enquirer* for making up stories, and I just assumed it had blown up one of the "I'm not feeling well" episodes into what appeared to me to be a libelous piece of trash. I never imagined it would be able to use truth as its defense.

Since just a few days earlier Kitty had told me that Gilda was feeling better, and Gilda sounded fine the next time we talked, I did not even think of mentioning the article to her. I was sure it was so scurrilous it would upset her.

The newspaper story really unhinged Pat, and she, like millions of Americans, was thrilled to read about Gilda's recovery in her inspiring cover story a few months later, in March 1988, in *Life* magazine. The *Life* story floored me because I had never really believed she was so sick in the first place. Of course, after reading the *Life* story—a stirring, upbeat account of her recovery—I believed the whole thing, and I was devastated. I made all sorts of excuses to myself. I had spent the previous year making films on an insanely intense schedule and had been commuting from New York to Philadelphia and Washington almost daily, and even though I owed her a letter I had barely had even a moment to write or call poor Gilda, whom I considered practically my oldest and best friend. I then tried to phone her many times. The phone rang and rang. It was very ominous.

Her book describes this entire period in excruciating detail. Crystal-clear is the message that until the end she maintained the soul of a poet.

Even when she was at the maximum point of her suffering, she remembered her friends and still tried to make them feel good.

THANKS FOR THE LOVE FOR ALL THESE YEARS

That was Gilda's inscription on the last card I ever received from her. It was her 1988 Christmas card, showing her, Gene, and Sparkle on their couch in Connecticut. For some curious reason Gilda sent me two Christmas cards that year. Gilda is wearing a scarlet sweater. Gene is wearing a zip-up sweatshirt of almost the identical color. He is holding Sparkle, who appears to be wearing a tiny little crown, or perhaps a flower in her hair. Gilda's arm is outstretched, her hand uplifted at a forty-five-degree angle, as if to say, "Here we are." In fact, her card does say, in her rounded handwriting with beloved nibbed pen:

> Here we are—Thanks for the letter—and the love
> for all these yrs.
>
> Gilda Gene Sparkle

In the letter she refers to, I had suggested she try a really radical cancer therapy: *chi kung*, a Chinese method of breathing and walking exercise that has reportedly had good success with cancer patients, especially ovarian cancer patients like Gilda.

I had also mentioned it to her on the phone a few weeks earlier. It had been a difficult conversation, both of us trying to maintain a sense of humor:

"Gilda, I think of you saying 'Bunny! Bunny!' on the first of every month."

"Bunny! Bunny! God, Dave, you remember that."

She was able to muster a chuckle, the last time I ever heard her laugh. Then she said something that completely unnerved me:

"Dave, I have to tell you. 'Bunny! Bunny!' doesn't work."

It was a big admission for her. The spiritual tremblings of her approaching death had forced her to throw out the beliefs and comforts of her whole life. As previously noted, she had always been mildly superstitious in the unconscious Jewish way, saying "kine-ahora," "God willing," "spit in your pocket," and the like, so as "not to tempt the fates," as she put it. She strongly believed that God loved a good joke and would protect the jokester as the apple of His eye. But she had realized that in spite of all her efforts, all her beliefs, all her wishes, all her wit—Father Time had left his calling card and put his big rough hand upon her ovaries, and she did not know the meaning of contentment anymore.

After her picture appeared on the cover of *Life*, Gilda in her last days went into a sort of tragicomic overdrive. She valiantly maintained her sense of humor. But she also maintained her customary sense of reality.

During this trying period Pat managed to get through to Gilda on the telephone, and she took the humorous approach.

"I called her and told her that her 'Yasir Arafat' look was her best hair since I'd known her," Pat said.

Pat had been lucky to get through to Gilda on one of her "ten good days." When she was undergoing radiation and chemotherapy, her months were divided into a cycle that sounded like it came from the evil witch's spell in some terrible old fairy tale. She had ten relatively good days, then ten days in quivering fear, then ten days in pain and suffering.

While she described this vividly in her book, she did not mention that, among other things, she began to throw what she called "tragedy teas" for herself and friends who were also having certifiably hard times. They were misery-loves-company affairs usually held at her house in Connecticut. Only the sore afflicted were allowed to attend. Gilda invited O'D to one of these because she, Pat, had recently had a "bad Pap" and was going through her own cancer scare. Anne Beatts was invited after her fiancé had had his head cut off in a helicopter accident.

It was at one of these teas that Gilda wrote the following verse, on doctors:

> Doctors are whippersnappers in ironed white
> coats
> Who spy up your rectums and look down your
> throats
> And press you and poke you with sterilized tools
> And stab at solutions that pacify fools.
> I used to revere them and do what they said
> Till I learned what they learned on was already
> dead.

Pat never got to attend her "tragedy tea." Gilda's invitation was suddenly canceled by the canceler of all. The rain came down in torrents on May 24, 1989, in Connecticut as a small family group gathered for Gilda's funeral.

Gilda once wrote she wanted to be buried with a working television set, and her epitaph to read:

GILDA RADNER PROGRAM INTERRUPTED DUE TO TECHNICAL DIFFICULTIES.

"I want to make sure anybody passing by my grave gets a good laugh . . . a good deep mortal laugh . . . even if I don't hear it," she joked.

Since her death, Gene Wilder and Joel Siegel, whose wife also succumbed early to cancer, have, in Gilda's name, sponsored new chapters and spin-offs of the Wellness Community, to be set up in various cities. Gene has been very active in alerting women to the signs of ovarian cancers and the methods of early detection. He took out a full-page ad in *People* magazine, in which he noted:

"My wife Gilda was afraid of cancer all her life. And even with wonderful doctors, no one discovered she had ovarian cancer until it was too late because they weren't looking for it.

"We also didn't know three of her relatives had died of it. And that was important, because a family history greatly increases a woman's chance of getting it. . . ."

ENVOI

Oh, Gilda! You left us with a bad ending for your story! It's too raw. Too tragic. Oh, it has finality, of course! No question about that! But what about poetic justice? You did not deserve all this cruelty, all this tragedy. You were the best and wisest woman I have ever known. You have left us inconsolable, by the loss of your voice, your presence which never once failed to make us feel good and fine and beautiful with laughter.

By prowling among your artifacts, by scenting your traces, by recalling and immersing myself in your sweet, gentle life and your painfully tragic end, I have come to know you and love you as never before. But I have not been able to solve the mystery of your death.

At least I have created in myself, and perhaps in others who loved you, an inner feeling that reminds me of one of your favorite poems, one of those we used to recite out loud at the top of our voices, especially the refrain—do you remember?

It went on for at least fifteen stanzas, which I am reciting to you out loud right now. But you understand—I have to spare the audience, for dramatic purposes. So let's let them overhear, in our best old stage whisper, just a fragment, adapted slightly:

With Apologies to Anonymous

Mourn, all ye Groves, in darker Shades be seen,
Let Groans be heard where gentle Winds have
been:
Ye *Detroit* River, weep your Fountains dry,
And all ye Plants your Moisture spend and die;
Ye melancholy Flowers, which once were Men,
Lament, until you be transformed again,
Let every Rose pale as the Lily be,

And Winter Frost seize the Anemone:
But thou, O Hyacinth, more vigorous grow,
In mournful Letters thy sad Glory show,
Enlarge thy Grief, and flourish in thy Woe:
For *Gilda*, the beloved *Gilda*'s dead,
Her Voice is gone, her tuneful Breath is fled.

Come, all ye Muses, come, adorn the Shepherd's Hearse,
With never-fading garlands, never-dying Verse.

Fair Galatea too laments thy Death,
Laments the ceasing of thy tuneful Breath:
Oft she, kind Nymph, resorted heretofore
To hear thy artful Measures from the shore:
Nor harsh like the rude *Belushi*'s were thy Lays,
Whose grating Sounds did her soft Ears displease:
Such was the force of thy enchanting Tongue,
That she for ever could have heard thy Song,
And chid the Hours that do so swiftly run,
And thought the Sun too hasty to go down,
Now does that lovely Nereid for thy sake
The Sea, and all her Fellow-Nymphs forsake.
Pensive upon the Beech, she sits alone,
And kindly tends the Flocks from which thou'rt gone.

Come, all ye Muses, come, adorn the Shepherd's Hearse,
With never-fading garlands, never-dying Verse. . . .

and so on forever.

Index